Novel Preaching

Also from Westminster John Knox Press by Alyce M. McKenzie

Matthew (Interpretation Bible Studies)

The Parables for Today

Preaching Proverbs: Wisdom for the Pulpit

Novel Preaching

*Tips from Top Writers
on Crafting Creative Sermons*

Alyce M. McKenzie

WJK WESTMINSTER
JOHN KNOX PRESS
LOUISVILLE · KENTUCKY

First edition
Published by Westminster John Knox Press
Louisville, Kentucky

10 11 12 13 14 15 16 17 18 19—10 9 8 7 6 5 4 3 2 1

Unless otherwise indicated, Scripture quotations are from the New Revised Standard Version of the Bible, copyright © 1989 by the Division of Christian Education of the National Council of the Churches of Christ in the U.S.A., and are used by permission.

A portion of the sermon "Filled with Fear" appears in Alyce M. McKenzie's *Hear and Be Wise: Becoming a Preacher and Teacher of Wisdom* (Nashville: Abingdon Press, 2004), 54–59. It is used by permission of Abingdon Press.

Book design by Sharon Adams
Cover design by Lisa Buckley
Cover image © Images.com/Corbis

Library of Congress Cataloging-in-Publication Data

McKenzie, Alyce M.,
  Novel preaching : tips from top writers on crafting creative sermons / Alyce M. McKenzie.
    p. cm.
  Includes bibliographical references and index.
  ISBN 978-0-664-23322-8 (alk. paper)
  1. Preaching. 2. Imagination—Religious aspects—Christianity. 3. Creative writing—Religious aspects—Christianity. I. Title.
  BV4211.3.M355 2010
  251.01—dc22

                                                                    2009028359

PRINTED IN THE UNITED STATES OF AMERICA

∞ The paper used in this publication meets the minimum requirements
of the American National Standard for Information Sciences—Permanence
of Paper for Printed Library Materials, ANSI Z39.48-1992.

Westminster John Knox Press advocates the responsible use of our natural resources. The text paper of this book is made from 30% post-consumer waste.

To Ben, Diane, Eston, Gayle, Kai, and Wally,
the "Significant Others" whose wise advice helped shape this book

Contents

Introduction

Suppose you go to the doctor for a checkup. Suppose that the doctor examines you and then says, "I am writing you a prescription that I want you to have filled immediately. Never mind why. Just trust me that it will improve your condition so that you will achieve optimal health." Then suppose the doctor, after shaking your hand briskly, leaves the room. I don't know about you, but there is no way I would have the prescription filled immediately. My mind would be too full of questions I deserve to have answered first. *What is wrong with me? What is this prescription supposed to do? What does optimal health mean for me?*

This book offers prescriptions from creative writers and teachers of preaching for cultivating and using the imagination in the preparation of sermons. As a reader, you have every right to say, "Before I get in the line at the pharmacy window, I deserve answers to a couple of key questions. What is our condition as preachers that requires this prescription? What effect will this advice have on our preaching if we take it? And what will be the signs that the prescription is improving the condition of our sermons?"

Diagnosis: Divided Identity

In the fourth book of *On Christian Doctrine*, Augustine states that the preacher should "pray and strive that he be heard intelligently, willingly, and obediently." The preacher achieves this end by "spurning none of these three things: that is, to teach, to delight, and to persuade."[1] The functions of teaching and delighting have continually divorced, remarried, and divorced again in every century.[2] The purpose of this book is to offer the antidote that can unite these two roles of preaching and

1

help them work and play well together.[3] It is the imagination. This book shows how preachers can cultivate imagination in daily life, and how they can use it to shape sermons that touch the emotions, inform the mind, and abide in the memory.

Not surprisingly, the book draws on the thought of contemporary teachers of preaching who have reflected on the role of imagination in the preparation of sermons. They have much to teach us about imaginative approaches to Scripture and shaping of sermons. But it also seeks advice from creative writers. Who better to advise us than literary artists who fashion narratives that invite readers to identify with characters and events and emerge transformed? Who better to turn to than a group of people whose vocation is using their imaginations in the close observation of the imagery, metaphors, and stories within them and around them?

We need advice on using our imaginations to mediate the divide between teaching and delighting in our preaching, because preaching today is living a double life with a double identity: teaching or entertainment. One identity says, "My name is teaching." This is the "six points and a PowerPoint" school of preaching. Pastors of many large, non-denominational churches insist that their flock doesn't know the basic beliefs of their faith. Many have turned to lengthy topical sermons, whose bulleted points appear on the PowerPoint screen behind them. The other identity says, "My name is experience." Such preaching banishes the teaching function of sermons to the Sunday school class or the blog. This approach is favored by some, though by no means all, contemporary worship advocates and emerging church practitioners. It uses story and imagery to connect with the emotions and experiences of contemporary people. Then there are the rest of us preachers, who may be clinging to the pendulum as it swings back and forth from sermon to sermon—in one sermon swinging toward teaching that can become tedious and in the next traveling back toward entertainment that may lack depth.

Medical History

Medical doctors ask for medical histories of their patients before they prescribe treatment. So here is the medical history, so to speak, of the great divide between teaching and engaging emotions in preaching. This current double sermonic life is only the latest outcrop of a malady that has plagued preaching in every century. The split between reason and imagination in Christian preaching began when the gospel spread to the Greco-Roman world. The expectations of non-Jewish audiences were shaped by several centuries of rhetorical training—the art of persuasive public address—perfected by Greek and Roman teachers. They drummed into their young students' heads that speeches should teach, delight, and persuade.[4] Unfortunately, these teachers divided reason from imagination, relegating the former to teaching and persuading and the latter to delighting. It was the function of the content, the logical argument, to teach and persuade. It was the function of style, word choices, and flourishes of delivery to delight. Metaphor and imagery were seen as ornamental, as sugar sprinkled on ideas to make the medicine go down.

This great divide between reason and imagination has influenced centuries of preachers to separate images, story, and metaphor from ideas, concepts, and lines of thought. The three-points-(each illuminated by an anecdote)-and-a-poem sermon is the descendant of persuasive speech in the rhetorical tradition of the ancient Greeks and Romans. This "three-points" sermon form has reincarnated itself in every century since then. It deserves to be one among many options for shaping a sermon, but not the only one.

In offering this brief diagnosis and medical history regarding preaching's double identity, I realize that I am not the only doctor in town. You are free to seek a second opinion and a third to diagnose preaching's malady and prescribe a treatment. I already know what they'll tell you if you want to save time and gas money driving all around town.

Second opinion: People are easily bored. They need sermons with stories and images.

For the past thirty-plus years many teachers of preaching have been saying, in effect, "We need more imaginative preaching, because people are bored with three points and a poem."

I remember sitting in church in high school bored by the predictability of three-point, deductive preaching, where the preacher tells you what he is going to tell you, tells you, then tells you what he has told you. About the time I sat restlessly in the pew, Fred Craddock was publishing his little book *As One without Authority*. It was the answer to a bored teenager's prayers. It reflected Craddock's struggle to teach preaching in the late 1960s and early 1970s, when authority was in question in every sphere of life, including the pulpit. It reflected what has come to be called a postmodern perspective, which looked favorably on the imagination and looked with suspicion on the claims of individual reason to discern and proclaim objective, one-size-fits-all truths.

Craddock advised preachers to stop going on the weekly white-water rafting ride of biblical interpretation and bringing the congregation back a key chain from the gift shop. Instead, he suggested they invite the congregation along for the inductive ride in sermons that share with the people the preacher's journey of discovery. Craddock's book pushed the preaching pendulum into a swing away from teaching and toward delighting.

Another book that came out at roughly the same time was Eugene Lowry's *The Homiletical Plot*. It highlighted the dynamic of conflict as the key to listener engagement and suggested a sermon form or plot that began with pointing out a conflict or discrepancy in life or text, intensifying it, then offering the textual, theological resolution and its implications for daily living.

Many preachers, in what came to be called the "new homiletic" of the 1980s and 1990s, embraced inductive, narrative-shaped sermons that made use of the imagery and literary forms of texts. Although teaching was not a primary concern, a number of "new homileticians" acknowledged that preaching needed a message that spoke to the mind as well as the senses.[5] The new homiletic was wary of directives from the preacher that, it felt, often tended to be heavy-handed and unnecessary.[6] Its practitioners believed that listeners, out of their common stock of knowledge of the Bible and Christian beliefs, and out of their common humanity, could do the work of applying indirect, aesthetically appealing messages to their lives.

Third opinion: People today yearn for knowledge about Scripture and their faith. They need sermons that teach.

Since the late 1990s, many preachers have been saying, "We can't assume that everybody has the biblical knowledge to apply our inductive sermons to their own lives, as preachers assumed they could in the 1970s. We need more deductive teaching sermons, because many people are not well informed about the Bible and their faith traditions."

These preachers are absolutely on target in their insistence that we need to teach in our sermons today. Historically, Christian preaching has turned up the volume on its teaching when other, contradictory teachings in the culture have set up their loudspeakers around its pulpits.[7] Today these challengers include biblical literalism, prosperity preaching, and nationalism wearing a mask of Christianity. Preaching's challengers also include the explosion of technology (*techne*) and the erosion of wisdom (*phronesis*) that leave many people pursuing a patchwork brand of faith. They piece together mismatched swatches of insights from self-help authors and other religions. The result is a faith that lacks both depth and breadth.[8]

Prescription: Sermons with Imagination

People are easily bored; at the same time, they crave knowledge about the Bible and their faith tradition. They need sermons that teach with imagination.

Back in the 1960s, novelist John Gardner remarked that "Real art is not in the sermon we hear in church on Sunday morning. . . . It is in the arches and the light."[9] I take that pejorative statement as a challenge. I have no doubt that you and I are up for it. We can incorporate both the arches and the light into the sermon.

I've been thinking for over fifteen years, ever since the day I walked in late to my graduate seminar in biblical interpretation at Princeton Theological Seminary, about writing a book on how we can cultivate our imaginations for preaching. The half dozen other students seated at the seminar table were passing around a sign-up sheet with dates and topics for our next paper: interpreting a genre of Old Testament literature for preaching. By the time I held the sheet in my hands, Psalms had been taken. The prophetic literature had been taken. The historical narratives had been taken. The only blank space awaiting a name was the one next to Proverbs. Nobody wanted them.

Neither did I, but, as we all know, the late bird doesn't get the worm. That evening, after I put the kids to bed, I sat down in my old red brocade chair and, with more duty than delight, began to read the book of Proverbs. "The crucible is for silver, and the furnace is for gold, but the LORD tests the heart" (17:3). "A cheerful heart is a good medicine, but a downcast spirit dries up the bones" (17:22). "Go to the ant, you lazybones; consider its ways, and be wise" (6:6).

Delight began to well up within me as I read on, and the insight dawned upon me that these sages, these teachers of wisdom, knew there was no need to make a false choice between teaching the mind or touching the emotions. I read a couple of proverbs to my young daughter the next day, and she said, "That's what everybody knows, in words you can see." And from the lips of a first-grader came the key to how the Israelite sages produced these bite-size ethical lessons that both satisfy our reason and speak to our emotions.

The writers of Proverbs distilled their observations of repeated patterns in life around them into brief word pictures. The source of their genius is the same as that of novelists: the habit of attentiveness. A few nights later I was reading 1 Kings 3, a passage in which a newly anointed, uncertain King Solomon gets to ask for whatever he wants from God.

He asks God for a "discerning mind." A footnote told me that another possible rendering of the Hebrew (*leb shomea*) was "a listening heart." I remembered that, in Hebrew thought, the heart was the seat, not just of emotion, but also of reason, imagination, and decision making.

The listening heart is a hyperattentiveness to everything around us with everything within us. It was the secret of how the Israelite sages taught in "words you can see," reaching the reason and evoking emotion, a method followed by a first-century rabbi named Jesus. "Why do you see the speck in your neighbor's eye, but do not notice the log in your own eye?" (Matt. 7:3).

It struck me that the listening heart is the work of the faculty we call the imagination, the antennae we have out for the particulars of the text, the cultural landscape, and our own spiritual "inscape." A thought meandered across my mind as I read 1 Kings 3—like a floater sometimes crosses our field of vision and disappears, to return at some unspecified time. My thought was, "Someday, someone should write a book about how preachers can cultivate a listening heart so they can preach sermons that use word pictures to inform the mind and transform the emotions. And they should consult with creative writers."

I went on to teach homiletics, first at Princeton Theological Seminary and now at Perkins School of Theology, and to write several books and numerous articles on preaching wisdom themes and texts. Along the way I read for pleasure the works of novelists, as well as a number of books on the craft of fiction writing. I also discovered the work of teachers of preaching over the past thirty years, and their wisdom for cultivating and incorporating the imagination in sermons.

So here is my prescription for preaching's divided identity. People are easily bored at the same time that they crave knowledge. But the prescription we offer as preachers isn't stories or bullet points. It is imagination. It is sermons that activate the power of the imagination to teach the mind and engage the emotions and will. The more people need basic teaching, the more our sermons need for it to be presented in imaginative ways.

A preacher who wants to engage listeners' interest and teach them biblical themes and theological beliefs had better befriend her imagination. People's lives have been profoundly shaped by the visual culture in which we live, in which images reign on TV, movies, and the Web. Cultural historian Richard Kearney, in his intriguing book *The Wake of Imagination: Ideas of Creativity in Western Culture*, portrays people today as pelted by a plethora of media images. Then he makes an astute comment that ought to make preachers' ears perk up. One of the greatest paradoxes of contemporary cultures, he writes, is that "at a time when the image reigns supreme the very notion of a creative human imagination seems under mounting threat. We no longer appear to know who exactly produces or controls the images which condition our consciousness."[10]

People learn through images in our culture. Images have the power to shape our personal and social lives, and many of them run contrary to the gospel.[11] We can't counter images with ideas alone. We need to counter them with other images.

Not only do people learn through images, but they also learn in interactive ways. It stands to reason that addressing our congregation with an abstract monologue is not the wisest strategy. Our listeners need sermons that, like life and the Bible, are both deep and delightful. They need sermons that teach, but not by listing abstract points with an occasional anecdote. They need sermons that lead with imagery, metaphor, and story, the domain of the imagination, and that allow ideas, teaching moments, and pertinent information, to arise from them. Sermons can only do that if the preacher, in preparing the sermons, has allowed God to work through his imagination, unleashed on the rich sensory realm of the text as it intersects the rich sensory realms of his congregation's daily lives and his own inward life.

This book will teach you, aided by the advice of creative writers and creative teachers of preaching, how to cultivate your imagination to observe your inner life, the life of your congregation, and the life of the biblical text: the inscape, the landscape, and the textscape. It will teach you how to use what you have cultivated to shape your sermons so that they both teach and delight.

Part 1 deals with "Cultivating the Imagination," while part 2 addresses "Shaping the Sermon." Chapter 1 invites readers to sit on the porch at a fictitious writer's workshop to gain the wisdom of fiction writers on cultivating the habit of close observation of inward and outward experience (referred to as a "knack for noticing"). Chapter 2 asks the question "Noticing What?" alerting the reader to patterns of character, scene, and imagery in text, inner life, and everyday life. Chapter 3 addresses the question "Noticing How?" and offers specific disciplines for fine-tuning the preacher's attention.

Part 2, "Shaping the Sermon," contains three chapters. Chapter 4, "Sermon Shapes," offers advice on shaping the sermon from fiction writers. Chapter 5 invites the reader to a sermon chefs' event in which various preachers prepare their favorite creative sermon recipes. Chapter 6 offers several sermons of my own from recent years, not as pristine, perfect examples of the book's principles, but as imperfect efforts of my recent past.

A friend told me about someone he knows who smokes but who, when he travels, always requests a nonsmoking room because he doesn't like the smell of the smoking rooms. Then he smokes in the room. Preachers who don't like to be bored ourselves but who bore others in our sermons are like that man. We preachers need theological depth to grow in our faith. When we don't offer it to others in our sermons, we are like that man. I say we open up the windows and let the fresh breath of imagination blow through.

Part 1

Cultivating the Imagination

Chapter One

A Knack for Noticing

Advice from Fiction Writers for Preachers

My dad, Robert H. Fowler Sr., was a newspaper and magazine publisher and author of eight historical novels. Until his death in 2002, he regularly challenged me with the question, "Why don't you start writing novels?"

I always had my answer ready. "I'm waiting until I have more life experience." The older I got, the less credible that excuse became, until finally I was forced to face the real reason. I don't write novels because I don't feel called to write novels. Thank God lots of other people do, though, because, as a preacher, I need to learn from them. And so do you.

In this chapter, I consult with creative writers about their methods for cultivating the imagination for writing short stories and novels and apply these methods to our preaching task. I pick the writers' brains for the answers to questions like, What kinds of details about daily life should we preachers be noticing? How can we develop the knack for noticing them?

Along the way, we'll also hear from a number of preachers and homileticians whose specific advice about preaching echoes these same ideas. After we've consulted with creative writers and teachers of preaching on how to cultivate our imaginations through careful observation, we'll discover (in chapters 3 and 4) how they then use what they have observed to shape their stories, novels, and sermons.

Before we go any further, I want to make clear what this chapter is not. It is not a historical survey of literary theory and the imagination. Nor is it a comprehensive review of prose fiction writers of the past two centuries. It is not a survey of how contemporary novelists conceive of the purpose of their art (though that one is really tempting) or a polling of explicitly religious novelists on how they express their faith through their fiction. It is not a compendium of examples from literature that you can use in your sermons. If you feel inspired by reading the chapter to travel down any of those fruitful avenues, by all means, follow your inclinations.[1]

I'm switching on the street lamps now for the path that lies ahead of us in this chapter. The chapter first describes the piece of meta-advice that almost every creative writer mentions: that we be attentive to life within us and around us. The chapter then outlines the three obstacles to that attentiveness: lack of daring (the desire to avoid pain that comes with the close observation of life within and without), lack of direction (not knowing exactly what to be attentive to), and lack of discipline (not being willing to cultivate the imagination through specific disciplines).

After a description of what creative writers mean by "attentiveness," the chapter focuses on creative writers' advice on what we ought to be noticing. Then comes their advice on disciplines for remembering and recording what we have noticed.

I think that you and I should go to a writer's conference together sometime. I know you are busy and may need some convincing that this time would be well spent, so here is my brief pitch as to the relevance of learning some fiction writing principles to your preaching task.

The Relevance of Fiction Writing Principles to Preaching

Novels and sermons are exercises in imagination. Sermons and novels are different genres of communication, but both require the use of the imagination. The methods involved in producing a private, written medium like novels are instructive for a public, spoken medium like sermons.

"Fiction" originally came from the Latin and meant "something shaped, molded, or devised."[2] We use it to refer to prose stories based on the interaction of an author's imagination with his or her surroundings. The essence of fiction is narration, the relating or recounting of a sequence of events or actions. Works of fiction usually focus on one or a few major characters who undergo some kind of change as they interact with other characters and deal with problems.[3]

The novel, though written, has oral antecedents and components. Today's sermons, though spoken, depend on prior study of written material—biblical text and secondary sources.[4] The antecedents of the novel lie in the oral performances of epic, heroic tales, which were crucial to preserving the collective memory of cultures before the advent of writing. Although the precursors of the novel preceded the printing press, the novel's proliferation as a literary form was made possible by the technology that allowed for the dissemination of mass copies of these extended written narratives.

Novels, though now a mass-produced, written medium, depend on what were originally forms characteristic of oral communication (imagery, vivid scenes, memorable characters, repeated themes, and exciting story lines) to connect with readers. As sacred literature, the same can be said of the Bible. Novels are a literary form with oral roots. As novelist John Gardner put it, "True fiction is, in effect, oral storytelling written down and fixed, perfected by revision."[5]

Novels and sermons are invitations to enter into a story. Now more than ever, people need to be drawn into a coherent story that is bigger than the disjointed episodes of our distracted lives. Much of the narrative preaching proposed over the past generation of homiletical theory assumes that people are, with their imaginations, creating a coherent narrative out of the events of their lives and that we can, as preachers, simply connect aspects of their story with the Bible's story. But some observers claim that people today aren't creating holistic narratives out of the disparate events of their daily lives. Rather, they are immersed in the episodic experiences of life with neither the skills nor the desire to look beyond them. In a recent essay, preacher, author, and homiletics professor Thomas G. Long questions whether people in our attention-deficit, high-tech, visual culture have the skills or the will to be engaged in an ongoing process of making a story of their lives. He suggests, rather, that many people are living in "random bursts," "our attention fleeting from *American Idol* to the troop movements in the Middle East to the desire to purchase a more powerful cell phone, a kind of cultural attention deficit disorder."[6]

Over twenty years ago, David Buttrick, in his book *Homiletic: Moves and Structures*, asserted that the biblical narrative of salvation provides an encompassing master story into which we can place our individual stories. The biblical narrative of salvation gives our often incoherent, episodic lives a new prelude and a new closing chapter.[7] His point may be pertinent now more than ever.

If people today don't have the skills to fashion a coherent narrative of their lives, why not turn to novelists, a group of people whose vocation is fashioning narratives inspired by their close observation of the people, places, and events of their daily lives? Why not consult with novelists whose passion is the creation of fictional worlds that invite readers to identification and transformation?

Novels and sermons begin with an openness to inspiration. A preacher seeks prayerfully to rely on the Holy Spirit when entering into a dialogue with a biblical text on behalf of the congregation. Often, we have the sense that our theme chooses us rather than the other way around. Many novelists have expressed a similar sense that their writing is a discovery more than an invention—that, in their work, they listen and allow characters, themes, and stories to emerge as much as or more than the novelists create them. There is a sense of receiving a gift in the way that many novelists speak of their creative flow. Annie Dillard says it well: "At its best, the sensation of writing is that of any unmerited grace. It is handed to you, but only if you look for it. You search, you break your heart, your back, your brain, and then—only then—it is handed to you."[8]

Julia Cameron describes the writing life as "being an open channel," affirming that "we can 'plug in' to the flow of writing rather than thinking of it as a stream of energy we must generate from within ourself."[9]

On the Porch

All right, that was my best shot. Now back to that writers' conference I'm hoping you'll attend with me. According to my online research, writers' conferences can take place in any number of settings. These include, but are by no means limited to, an airport Sheraton in Portland, Oregon; resorts in Maui; upscale hotels in Manhattan; retreat centers in the mountains of western North Carolina; and picturesque inns in Connecticut.

The Breadloaf Inn in Middlebury, Connecticut, looks quite scenic. Those Green Mountains would make a lovely backdrop for this chapter. The Breadloaf Writers' Conference, held every August since 1925 at the Breadloaf Inn, sounds a little daunting, though. The online description includes words like "rigorous" and mentions meetings with faculty, agents, and editors.

I say we keep a Breadloaf-like stage set, but imagine attending a lower-key, more laid-back event, the kind in which we lounge on a porch, put our feet on the railing, and nurse our beverage of choice. Because this is our imagination talking, any creative writer or novelist, dead or alive, can show up and hold court briefly, giving us mini-lectures and sound advice.

Be prepared to hear our creative writers focus on the importance of attentiveness. In my reading of numerous essays and books by creative writers about writing, this theme shows up again and again. I recently went to lunch with C. W. Smith, professor of English at Southern Methodist University and author of eight novels. He graciously fielded my barrage of questions about what and how preachers can learn from novelists. Something he said that stuck in my mind was, "As a teacher of creative writing, much of my time is spent in trying to get students to notice what they see. And then, the next step is to get them to trust that there may be some significance in their observations."

Now, if everybody is settled comfortably in their respective rocking chairs (the kind with comfortable cushions), let's begin by talking about attentiveness—not just seeing but noticing . . . or, as Professor Smith puts it, "noticing what you see."

A Brief Interruption

As we are settling into our chairs, an elderly but vigorous gentleman strides out of the inn to stand before us. He is wearing elbow patches (and a tweed jacket, too, of course) and a cape (my impression is that authors stereotypically wear capes), a beret, jeans, and high-top red sneakers. He has lustrous gray hair, swept straight back from his brow. He has suspiciously good posture for a man his age. He has mistaken us for the continuing education class from the local community college for which he has agreed to do a guest lecture on the history of the novel.

Before I can stop him, he begins to speak in that pseudo-British accent so often adopted by announcers on luxury car commercials.

"Like the imagination, the novel has always had its fans and its detractors. Its detractors have caricatured it as a distraction from serious reflection. Its defenders have insisted it can help readers interpret life, not just escape from it."[10] He pauses and frowns at us as if to ask, "Why aren't any of you taking notes?" Then he continues.

"In the late 1600s, the novel grew out of the heroic epic featuring larger-than-life figures like Charlemagne and King Arthur.[11] As the genre gained momentum in the eighteenth century with the work of Joseph Fielding, Daniel Defoe, and Samuel Richardson, novels focused on more ordinary lives with details generated by the imagination of the authors."

Because this is actually sort of interesting, some of us lean forward attentively.

With a nod of approval at us, he proceeds. "As the novel entered the nineteenth century, the novel's defenders pointed out that, in its realistic depiction of everyday lives, it could convey moral insights. The work of Jane Austen, Anthony Trollope, George Eliot, William Makepeace Thackeray, Charles Dickens, Honoré de Balzac and Leo Tolstoy are examples of the realistic novel.[12] The school of literary naturalism was an offshoot of realism. It was championed by French writer Émile Zola, who saw the novel's purpose as depicting real lives of prostitutes and laborers, not moralizing (1840–1902)."

Due to his animation about his subject, we have now begun to wonder how we could possibly have lived this long without knowing these things.

"The school of Impressionism among novelists, inspired by the work of impressionist painters Claude Monet (1840–1926) and Edgar Degas (1834–1917), focused on immediate physical sensation rather than explanatory summary. The novel's purpose was, not to convey lessons, but to evoke the inner life of a character. As an example, consider Virginia Woolf and her stream of consciousness approach."[13]

A couple of us are taking notes now, which seems to energize him.

"In the mid-twentieth century, the school of New Criticism has insisted that the work of art is a self-contained entity. The author's intention and social conditions are not relevant. Reader response criticism in the sixties said it's the reader who finalizes or actualizes a work as much as the author. Deconstructionist and postmodernist theories of the novel's purpose aren't concerned with the ethical, moral impact of novels on readers.[14] John Gardner, a leading figure in the New Fiction school of the 1960s, understood fiction as morally enlivening and humanity-enhancing."[15]

He pauses now, and gestures dramatically. "Regardless of what the critics say the purpose of the novel should or should not be, no one can take from the novelist her own sense of purpose in creating a unique work, and no one can take from the reader the impact it has on him."

Our lecturer concludes with a flourish: "There is nothing to stop a novelist from embracing, as many do, the purpose of expanding the perspective of readers, inviting them into an alternate universe in which their values are affirmed and challenged as they identify with the people and events of the narrative."

I rise to my feet to thank him, but the teacher of the class he was supposed to be addressing has already taken him by the elbow and is leading him to the other side of the porch where they are waiting for him.

The Habit of Attentiveness: A Knack for Noticing (KFN)

Now back to what we were about to discuss before our interruption: attentiveness, which will hereafter be referred to as KFN (Knack for Noticing). Fiction writers and preachers need, not just to see, but to notice. We need, not just to walk by life with glazed eyes, but to hone in on daily

sensory details, noting and recording them for future uses we can't yet predict. We need to pay attention to our inner life (inscape), life around us (landscape), and the life of the biblical text (textscape). Natalie Goldberg,   *Preaching begins not with expression,*
in her book *Writing Down the Bones,*   *but with impression.*
calls this "composting": "We collect   —*Fred Craddock*
experiences, and from the decomposi-
tion of the thrown-out eggshells, spinach leaves, coffee grinds, and old steak bones of our minds come nitrogen, heat, and very fertile soil. Out of this fertile soil bloom our poems and stories."[16]

Obstacles to KFN

Creative writers mention two obstacles to cultivating the imagination: a lack of discipline and a desire to avoid pain. I've added a third for us preachers: lack of direction. We aren't sure what we're supposed to be noticing. Thus, the three obstacles to KFN are

- Lack of discipline (not developing the habit of recording right away what we have noticed)
- Lack of daring (desire to avoid the pain that comes with noticing)
- Lack of direction (not knowing what to notice)

For the first obstacle to attentiveness, lack of discipline, an element of laziness can be the culprit. It takes work to be alert and even more to make note of what we've noticed for future use. The fact is that we are all abidingly resistant to developing and maintaining such habits. We assure ourselves that we'll remember the insight, the image, or the story that has just floated through our mind and write it down later. The truth is, we won't. Do not allow the insight you gain from observation to be lost due to laziness. Tag in your mind this maxim: There is no later. There is now or never.

Regarding the second obstacle to attentiveness, the desire to avoid pain, novelist Charles Johnson, author of *Middle Passages*, highlights emotional honesty as a prerequisite of creative writing. He cites novelist and teacher of writing John Gardner's advice to him that novelists need to "go to those places that are emotionally difficult to visit."[17] Preachers need to face head on the qualities within themselves they would rather not face and the issues in their congregations and communities that it would be easier not to address. If we have an ego struggle (and who doesn't?), we need to face it and name it. If our community thinks racism is not a problem because they are homogenous, we need to debunk that assumption.

Frederick Buechner insists in his fiction that we "face the darkness." By "darkness" he means "a sense of uncertainty, of being lost, of being afraid; . . . conflict between races, between nations, between individuals each pretty much out for himself when you come right down to it; . . . If we are people who pray, darkness is apt to be a lot of what our prayers are about. If we are people who do not pray, it is apt to be darkness in one form or another that has stopped our mouths."[18]

Attentiveness is a habit that requires courage. Japanese film director Akira Kurosawa says that to be an artist means never to avert your eyes. "That's difficult because we want to flinch. The artist must go into the white hot center of himself, and our impulse when we get there is to look away and avert our eyes."[19]

Attentiveness requires courage because it requires empathy, which itself is a form of imagination. Many novelists feel that the empathy to imagine others' lives is the genesis of fiction writing, that novelists create their characters by first becoming them.

Novelist and short story author Andre Dubus lost one leg and the use of the other in a 1986 accident. In an essay titled "Song of Pity," he tells of a cold winter afternoon, years before his accident, when he was a graduate student at the University of Iowa Writers' Workshop. He came upon a man in a wheelchair who was unable to continue up a steep incline, and Dubus pushed the man's chair the rest of the way. Years later, Dubus found himself in a wheelchair, and he reflects back on that afternoon: "I lacked imagination. Or I lacked the compassion and courage to imagine someone else's suffering. I never thought of my friend making his bed, sitting on a toilet, sitting in a shower, dressing himself, preparing breakfast and washing its dishes, just to leave the house, to go out into the freezing air of Iowa."[20]

As we sit on this sun-dappled porch at our writer's conference, all seems right with the world; but we know that life beyond our porch holds shadows because we've seen them. On the subjects of courage and honesty, Annie Dillard advises writers to "write as if you were dying. At the same time, assume you write for an audience consisting solely of terminal patients. That is, after all, the case. What would you begin writing if you knew you would die soon? What could you say to a dying person that would not enrage by its triviality?"[21]

Legend has it that the poet John Donne sometimes slept in a casket to remind himself of his mortality. While that seems extreme to me, an awareness of what awaits us in the future can heighten our attentiveness to what surrounds us in the present.

Creative writer and teacher Julia Cameron suggests an exercise for cultivating honesty. She calls it "The Flashlight." She describes it in this way:

> We begin by honestly asking questions. We answer until we arrive at honest answers. We can try sentences like:
>   "If I let myself admit it, I . . ."
>   "If it weren't so risky I would . . ."
>   "If it didn't scare me, I . . ."
>   "If it weren't so stupid, I'd . . ."
>   "If it weren't so threatening, I would admit . . ."
>   "If I let myself know it, I feel . . ."
>   "If I let myself feel it, I should . . ."
>   "If I let myself entertain the thought, I should . . ."
>   "I'm not ready yet, but eventually I need to . . ."[22]

Annie Dillard, in her book *The Writing Life*, quotes Anne Truitt, the sculptor: "The most demanding part of living a lifetime as an artist is the strict discipline of forcing oneself to work steadfastly along the nerve of one's own most intimate sensitivity."[23]

So lack of discipline and the reflex to avoid pain are two obstacles to attentiveness. A third may be that we don't quite know to what we are supposed to be attentive. A barrage of impressions make up the inscape, landscape, and textscape of the preacher's experience. What are we to notice?

KFN What? Noticing Floaters

Creative writers offer the following advice, loudly, clearly, and repeatedly: pay attention to the stray images, thoughts, and insights that come into your mind. I've baptized these stray thoughts "floaters," since they float through our minds like a floater sometimes swims across our screen of vision when our eyes are closed. I'm not talking about the kind of stray thoughts that call for the intervention in your life of a mental health professional or corrections officer. You should pay attention to them, too, but for different reasons.

I'm talking about stray impressions that have creative potential for a sermon, random thoughts or images that you experience when you are daydreaming at that endless stoplight. Hearing of the terminal illness of an acquaintance, I had a stray thought: I wondered if facing imminent death might force one to list all the things that one would never do, even if one lived forever. The people one would never befriend. The books one would never read. The languages one would never master.

Imagination does not take off on flights into fantasy but walks down the street.
—*Fred Craddock*

I was visiting a friend's father in the hospice wing of a local nursing home. On the way in and out I stopped and chatted with a couple of folks sitting in wheelchairs in the halls. They brightened up. They are used to people walking by them, I guess. The thought came to me, *I'm visiting my future self.* Stray thoughts.

Everybody has floaters. It's up to you, the preacher, taking a page from the novelist, to articulate and record your floaters, even though you don't know exactly how your thoughts will eventually come to fruition. When you are mulling over a sermon, immersed in the text and emerging theme, you've created a magnet that attracts the iron filings of your stray impressions, your floaters. Show them some respect. Pay attention to them, and get them down on paper.

On the porch at Breadloaf Inn, I rock back and forth in my chair and take out my notebook where I've recorded some floaters from the past couple of days. I noticed that a number of my neighbors are stringing Christmas lights outside their homes and that most of them are placed with precision and concern for a pleasing effect. But at one house at the end of the street, the homeowner appears to have tossed a tangled skein of lights up into his yard's lone, scraggly tree.

I was listening to a story on NPR on my drive home from school the other afternoon, a story about somebody getting a patent for a crustless

As God is primarily the Creator, so God's creation, humankind, is called to create, not merely called to be the object or the product of the divine imagination, but called to be a participant in that creative imagination.
—*J. Barrie Shepherd*

peanut butter and jelly sandwich. I thought about the value of that invention compared to, say, the lightbulb.

I was sitting in church on Sunday night in the alto section looking out over the people gathered to hear us as we were about to begin our performance of Handel's *Messiah*. Yesterday morning I had resented having to sit through a two-hour rehearsal. Tonight I was grateful I had. While I preached a sermon recently assuring people of "do overs," when the conductor raises his baton, the violins (and the altos) better be ready the first time.

And then it was time to stand and sing. "And the Glory, the glory of the Lord . . ."

These are floaters. Novelist Joyce Carol Oates wrote an entire essay in response to the question she says she always gets from the person seated next to her at dinner parties: "Why do you write?" Her answer, "I am obsessed with the deeps of the mind, of the imagination, particularly of the semi-conscious imagination, which throws up to us bizarre and lovely surprises daily and nightly. Those of us who 'write' . . . consciously arrange and re-arrange reality for the purposes of exploring its hidden meanings."[24]

Normally novelist Stephen King's mission in life is scaring the hell out of us. Several years ago, he took a break from this primary pastime to write a very insightful little book called *On Writing*, in which he gives us this piece of advice: "Let's get one thing clear right now, shall we? There is no Idea Dump, no Story Central, no Island of the Buried Bestsellers; good story ideas seem to come quite literally from nowhere, sailing at you right out of the empty sky: two previously unrelated ideas come together and make something new under the sun. Your job isn't to find these ideas but to recognize them when they show up."[25]

As a preacher, I believe the Holy Spirit works through our imaginations to help us identify these preachable tidbits. Most fiction writers talk more about the process of finding than the identity of the Sender. Science fiction writer Ray Bradbury teaches us, "Ideas lie everywhere, like apples fallen and melting in the grass for lack of wayfaring strangers with an eye and a tongue for beauty, whether absurd, horrific, or genteel."[26]

> *"Attending" is the art of paying attention, of tending to, and our tending can take many forms. We can tend a garden or a soup, a hearth or a baby. . . . Tending calls for watchfulness and vigilance; it calls for skill and care. More than anything, it asks us to stay awake, to keep watch, even when the night is long and we are sleepy disciples.*
> —Anna Carter Florence

> *Our experience as preachers is that the Spirit breathes into us and shakes us up when we become available and receptive to suggestions coming from "out of the blue."*
> —Linda Clader

We've been sitting on these wicker rocking chairs long enough to need to stand up and stretch our legs. Maybe walk around the grounds and see if you can pick up a couple of Bradbury's apples. When you come back, pick a different chair, just to see the porch from a fresh angle.

Types of Floaters

Here is a sampling of floaters that creative writers encourage us to notice, name, and capture for future use.[27] The first five are covered in this chapter. Subsequent chapters address the remainder of the list.

- Dilemma
- Incongruity that leads us to ask "Why?"
- Connection between two otherwise unrelated people, events, or situations
- Memory
- Common emotion
- Archetypal characters
- Flexible image or concept
- Imaginative situations
- Intriguing fictional situation

The Dilemma, or Catch-22. You find yourself or someone you know facing a situation for which there is no solution. Any action taken will be painful and will exact a great price. My sermon "Filled with Fear" in chapter 6 opens with a man who has two choices, a future of being alone or taking a risk to enter into a new relationship. Neither choice seems appealing to him. He is stuck. Joseph in the sermon "Joseph, the Father of Our Dreams," is facing a dilemma: reject Mary and subject her to humiliation, or raise a child that is not his own.

The Incongruity. You notice something that doesn't fit or make sense. A fiction writer would later use these incongruities as aspects of setting, plot, or character. You can start thinking like that as well. Suppose that you are driving down the highway and notice two stores next to each other: one is called "Boxes to Go," and the other is "Caskets Inc." You begin wondering about the odd juxtaposition of the two stores.

Suppose after a conversation with the harshest, most critical person you know, you wonder why he or she is also the one who is most sensitive to criticism.

Suppose you notice that a negative event leads to positive consequences. Maybe, for example, a blackout on a suburban block leads neighbors to come out of their houses and meet for the first time.

Noticing an incongruity leads immediately to asking "Why?" Novelist Antonya Nelson says most of her stories and novels begin with a "why" question that came to her mind in observing life or in her reading. "Why does the orderly try to lift the 326-pound dead woman alone? . . . Did the slave murder her master's son and, if so, why?"[28]

As I was mulling over the text for the sermon "My Favorite Angel" (Matt. 28:1–10), I noticed an incongruity. Angels always say, "Do not be afraid," when people are trembling in front of them. Why doesn't the angel in Matthew 28 comfort the distraught guards at the tomb (Matt. 28:4)?

As a teacher of preaching, I teach my students to ask "Why?" questions about Scripture. Why did only one of the ten lepers return to thank Jesus? Why did Jacob send everyone on ahead and sleep by himself by the river Jabbok? I'm going to start encouraging students to ask "Why?" questions about themselves and the people and events around them. *Why, even at this time of crisis, do I feel serene? Why is the candidate who lost the election not in a state of complete depression, but actually seems energized and ready for the next thing? Why is she so jealous of her coworker? Why are they building another mall when the old one sits empty?*

That kind of attentiveness to inner and outer stray thoughts could provide fodder for a sermon I preach in the future. When I come to Romans 5:3 where Paul says that "suffering produces endurance," I ask, "Why would he say that, when we know full well that it often produces bitterness?" Then I remember my former reflections, about my own inner life, about the candidate I observed, and I think about how, if at all, they may be connected.

The Connection. You notice a similarity in two events, people, places, or periods that are otherwise unrelated. Here we allow the imagination to do its metaphor- or analogy-making work. I was reading a newspaper editorial that my mother Beverly Conner wrote recently for her local paper, the *Patriot News*, in Harrisburg, Pennsylvania. It was titled, "Mudslinging isn't a new trend," on political criticism throughout American presidential elections. I learned that Mary Todd Lincoln was accused by some of being a traitor when her sister Emilie, whose Confederate husband had been killed in action, moved into the White House with her children. Here is a spark waiting to be struck between this historical situation and a contemporary one in which a political figure is accused of guilt by association.[29]

The "connection" is often sparked for preachers as we view our experiences, past and present, through the lens of a biblical text. In my sermon "Wisdom in Person," based on the "Ode to a Woman of Worth" (Prov. 31:10–31), I invite my audience of women clergy to connect their to-do lists with the to-do list of the woman in the passage.

I once preached a sermon on our calling as Christians sparked by a connection I discerned between the call stories of Moses (Exod. 4:10) and

Paul (2 Cor. 12:7–10). They both led with excuses. Moses said, in effect, "Lord, I have a weakness, take away my task." And Paul said, in effect, "Lord, I have a task, take away my weakness." They both prayed prayers that God didn't answer.

Amy Bezecny, a student in a course I taught called "Preaching Biblical Wisdom," spoke—in a sermon on Ecclesiastes 1:1–11 called "Turning Fully to God"—about how preachers ignore Ecclesiastes in their preaching. She said that it was like ordering "partial view" seats to a Broadway show or a baseball game. We have a partial view of the canon without Ecclesiastes' perspective. It may be cheaper, but you get what you pay for.[30]

Connections are a type of floater that preachers can conscript for sermons, just as they spark creative writers' novels and short stories.

The Memory. A certain sensory experience—sight, smell, sound, touch, taste—transports you back in time to something you did not think you remembered. Smells often have this effect. A novelist who explored the boundaries of this phenomenon is Marcel Proust in his *The Remembrance of Things Past.* A thousand pages are sparked by one crumbling cookie.

Two fruitful questions to ask a biblical text are, "What memories of the author and his or her community seem to lie beneath this text?" and "What memories of my own does this text spark?"

Chilean novelist Isabelle Allende, when asked how she suddenly became a novelist after a journalism career, attributed it to her respect for the power of memory:

> On January 8, 1981 . . . I heard that my grandfather was dying in Chile. He was the most important male figure in my life. . . . I began a letter. It was sort of a spiritual letter to say good-bye and tell him that he could go in peace because I had all the anecdotes that he had told me, all his memories with me. I had not forgotten anything. To prove that, to prove that life goes on and memory is important, I started writing the first anecdote he ever told me.

Five hundred pages later, she realized the letter had become a novel.[31]

Christina, my dental hygienist, told me about her adopted son Dennis, five years old, whom she adopted from an orphanage in the Soviet Union when he was two. For his third birthday, she decided to make a traditional Russian meal for him and told him enthusiastically, "Dennis, I'm making borscht for you!" He began crying inconsolably. He kept saying, "No Yetta. No Yetta." Trying to find some clue to his distress, she looked through the small photo album that had been with his things when they adopted him. There was a picture of Yetta, his caregiver at the orphanage, spooning borscht into his mouth as he sat in his high chair. He associated his new mother making borscht with being returned to the orphanage. He stopped crying when she said, "Dennis, you never have to eat borscht again."

According to novelist Toni Morrison,

> All water has a perfect memory and is forever trying to get back to where it was. Writers are like that: remembering where we were, what valley we ran through, what the banks were like, the light that was there, and the route back to our original place. It is emotional memory—what the nerves and the skin remember as well as how it appeared. And a rush of imagination is our "flooding."[32]

I use a lot of examples in my sermons from my own memory bank. I want to use experiences of my congregation (with their permission, of course) more fully. This honors the corporate, dialogical nature of preaching. Examples from Scripture, from the history of our nation and world, and from our religious tradition can be presented as memories from our common memory bank rather than randomly chosen anecdotes.

The Common Emotion. You experience a feeling that is either startlingly new to you or obsessively old.[33] It could be a negative emotion like jealousy that makes an unwelcome cameo appearance when you hear of a friend or coworker's promotion. It could be a positive emotion, like the joy I felt on discovering that the restaurant I had eaten in last Thursday had the credit card I had been looking for all afternoon at home. The thrill of finding it was worth the irritation of thinking it was lost. Fiction writers ascribe these emotions to fictional characters and brainstorm situations that would produce such feelings.

Novelist Melanie Rae Thon tells of reading about a man who may have killed his son. "He went into a blackout—he was drunk—and the child was dead when the man woke up the next day." He probably killed him but will never be sure. She says the stories in her short-story collection *First, Body* arose out of her probing the question, "If you're responsible for another person's suffering or death, how do you learn to see yourself with any kind of compassion?"[34]

For preachers, it's useful to tap into this emotional dynamic when studying a biblical text, asking ourselves, "What emotions seem to pervade this text, and what is my own response to this text?" Creative writers would encourage us to notice these common emotions in life within and around us and to journal about them. Then they become a part of the emotional repertoire we bring to future sermons.

Two common emotions that appear in my sermons in chapter 5 are a vague sense of fear ("Filled with Fear") and an expectation of failure and disappointment ("My Favorite Angel"). Both these emotions are negative. Maybe I need to develop my knack for noticing positive common emotions as I observe life, attentive to my inward reactions.

Chapter Two

Noticing What?

Characters and Plot

John Gardner alerts us to three key elements of fiction writing, all of which have many lessons for preachers. They are archetypal characters, flexible concepts or images, and imaginative situations.[1] These features of character and plot give us numerous clues for what to notice—and how to pay attention for the bud of imagination as it starts to grow within us.

Archetypal Characters

What Gardner calls "archetypal characters" abound in fiction. They are distinctive characters whose strengths and flaws shape the plots around them. Examples he gives are Raskolnikov from Fyodor Dostoevsky's *Crime and Punishment*, *Lolita* from Nabokov's novel of the same name, and Huck Finn from Mark Twain's novel *The Adventures of Huckleberry Finn*.[2] Creative writers encourage us to develop a knack for noticing repeated patterns of character, plots, and images in our inner and outer lives.

Toni Morrison uses the archetypal character of a tar baby in her novel of the same name. She began reflecting on the old story about the tar baby that a white man used to catch a rabbit and on the fact that "Tar Baby" is a name that white people called black children, especially girls. She discovered that there is a tar lady in African mythology and that "at one time a tar pit was a holy place, because tar was used to build things. . . . It held together things like Moses' little boat and the pyramids." Tar Baby in her novel becomes an archetypal character, "the black woman who can hold things together."[3]

In biblical texts, such characters abound. The preacher uses her imagination to brainstorm ways the character of archetypal biblical people connects with the characters of her people. How is it similar and different from ours? How might it shape ours?

Thinking of biblical people in this precise way is new for me. It's also new for me to think in this way about the contemporary people who appear in the stories in my sermons, both in this book and beyond it. But maybe my sermons and yours do include archetypal characters, both biblical and in our illustrative examples. This insight makes me want to be more attentive to archetypal characters, distinctive characters whose strengths and flaws shape the plots around them, in both Bible and life. It makes me want to reflect on the strong personalities around me in my daily life—on their distinctive qualities, good and bad, and how they shape the lives of those around them. This insight also makes me want to look at biographies and characters in novels I read through this lens of "archetypal character."

Flexible Images or Concepts

Novelists' art of observation often produces what Gardner calls "a flexible image or concept" that organizes a web of complex feelings and ideas. Examples Gardner gives are Ralph Ellison's *The Invisible Man*, Joseph Heller's *Catch-22*, and Alex Haley's *Roots*.[4] Some flexible images that show up in my sermons are "shouting stones" ("Silent Disciples, Shouting Stones"), light-filled graveyards ("My Favorite Angel"), and lost coins ("Tony, Tony, Turn Around").

Imagery means more than pictures; it includes the whole physical and sensory dimension of the world portrayed in a sermon.
—Patricia Wilson-Kastner

The Bible is filled with such images and concepts. Prominent examples include the parting of the Red Sea, the provision of manna in the wilderness, turning the water into wine, and the cross as a symbol, not just of brutality, but of divine redemption of that brutality. When we come to a text to discern a theme for a sermon, we seek to discern a "flexible image or concept that organizes the web of complex feelings and ideas" of the text. This discernment process is at the heart of the approaches of several contemporary homileticians we hear from in chapter 5.[5]

Imaginative Situations

Yet another fruit of novelists' attention to life around them is the imaginative situation. Examples include John Fowles's *The Collector* (lonely man holds his love interest captive), James Dickey's *Deliverance* (four men caught in a primitive, violent test of manhood), Goethe's *Faust* (bargain with the devil), Defoe's *Robinson Crusoe* (struggle to survive when isolated on an island), Washington Irving's *Rip Van Winkle* (a man waking up in the present to the loss of the past), and Ann Patchett's *Bel Canto* (a group of people in an extended hostage situation).

The imaginative situation grows out of the novelist's mulling over the characters and conflicts of those around her in the context of what's going on within her.

Screenplay writer Karl Iglesias says that producers look for a screenplay whose idea is "uniquely familiar" and which "promises conflict." He means that they want something unique (new, fresh, compelling) but with familiar events and emotions to which viewers can relate.[6] He gives a couple of examples: A teenager is mistakenly sent into the past, where he must make

> *For preachers, imagination is the ability to form images in the minds of their listeners that are not physically present to their senses, so that they find themselves in a wider world with new choices about who and how they will be.*
> *—Barbara Brown Taylor*

sure his mother and father meet and fall in love, or else he won't exist in the future (*Back to the Future*). Kidnappers nab the wife of a rich man and threaten to kill her if he doesn't pay a ransom. But he is delighted, and urges them to go ahead (*Ruthless People*).[7]

For the preacher, not only his life and that of his people, but also the Bible, are full of uniquely familiar situations that promise conflict. Uniquely familiar situations in the sermons in chapter 6 include the experience of facing someone you've wronged ("Getting What's Coming to You") and finding life where we expected only death ("My Favorite Angel"). Preaching invites listeners into the world of a biblical text, which always involves a uniquely familiar situation.

Canadian novelist Robertson Davies would call these uniquely familiar situations "archetypal situations." He says his own novels are full of them and that everybody experiences archetypes at some time or other:

> The thing about an archetype is that you have emotions and a strength of feeling which goes beyond what you can explain simply in terms of the situation. Sometimes people say, "I don't know why I am making such a fuss about this thing; it really isn't worth all that bother, is it? Then you know they're in the grip of an archetype; very frequently they're being dragged somewhere by a pattern of

feeling which is stronger than merely the surface of their emotion. The patterns are universal but they come freshly to our individual experience.[8]

Examples he gives include falling in love, being at a crossroads, and becoming uncharacteristically angry.

Evil

In a sort of grown-up, dead-serious version of the child's game "Where's Waldo?" short story and creative nonfiction writer Susan Neville advises us continually to ask the question, "Where is Iago?" Iago is the villain of Shakespeare's play *Othello*, who, by planting false suspicions in Othello's mind about his wife Desdemona, impels him to murder her in the marital bed. Iago creates dramatic tension.[9] He is a catalyst in the story. In every relationship and situation, says Neville, there are tensions that could either go on unresolved indefinitely or erupt into a story line. In the case of Othello's love for Desdemona, passion cohabits with suspicion, loyalty with doubt. In most relationships, scenes, and situations in life there is a hairline crack, a fault line. Iago is a metaphor for "the character or force whose function in the plot is to see . . . that fault line, to insert himself within it, . . . to become like water finding a fissure in stone and settling in, causing the stone to crack."[10]

Iago's motives are self-centered, his jealousy of Othello is for reasons real and imagined. Neville quotes Reinhold Niebuhr that "evil is always the assertion of some self-interest without regard to the whole."[11] A lesson Neville has learned from literature is that evil enters into human situations "through solipsism: one human being unable to see another human being as real." [12]

So the preacher, in observing situations around and within herself, as well as in the world of the biblical text, needs to ask the question, "Where is Iago here?" Where is the force of evil that threatens to crack open the scene, the situation, the relationship?

Theologian Mary Katherine Hilkert says the preacher's role is both to name grace and to name that which is not grace. There is a challenge here to all of us preachers to use our imaginations to see, smell, taste, hear, and touch the evil in life within and around us and in the biblical text. It is my love of comfort. It is the jealousy between two church staff members. I just finished writing an essay on Psalm 14 for a preaching journal; Psalm 14 is a cry for justice, probably from the postexilic period in Israel's history. "Have they no knowledge, all the evildoers who eat up my people as they eat bread, and do not call upon the LORD?" (Ps. 14:4).

Where is Iago in Psalm 14? He is in what one scholar labeled "practical atheism."[13] Iago is the little voice in the heads of the wealthy that tells them they can go on oppressing the poor with impunity, since God, while a reality, is not present or relevant.

How can we be on the lookout for Iago slithering through our Gardens of Eden? Susan Neville tells of attending a question-and-answer session after a talk by Thomas Keneally about the interviews he did with Holocaust survivors while writing *Schindler's List*. A student, deeply moved by the talk, asked, "What is the one thing I should do if I want to be an artist?" Keneally said, "Try if at all possible to see the evil that no one sees and that will be, in fifty years, the thing that no one can believe we did nothing about."[14]

Character, Plot, Scene, and Imagery

I don't know about you, but I'm tired of sitting again. Although I admit I find all this talk about evil oddly energizing, still, it seems time for a break. This might be a good time to stretch our legs and visit the snack table. They just put out more of those little spring rolls with the dip. I say we walk around the inn twice to burn them off before we eat them.

As we gather once again on the scenic porch, surrounded by the Green Mountains, we recap the morning so far. We've talked about the importance of attentiveness and identified three obstacles to cultivating it in our sermon preparation (that all start with the letter "D" no less): lack of discipline, lack of daring, and lack of direction. We've looked at several floaters that the imagination offers us to which we need to be attentive. They include dilemma, incongruity, connection, memory, common emotion, archetypal characters, flexible images and concepts, and uniquely familiar situations. We explored the need to be attentive to the presence of evil within, without, and in the text, as we played the "Where's Iago?" game.

Your consciousness is floating in its own unique sea of images. The sea is uniquely yours, but some of those images we share. Some of those images might grab me as a listener, and pull me into our world and the world of the Bible in riveting ways. Some of your images can unlock some of mine. Once that happens, we are communicating on a subliminal level, beneath the language of words, with symbols evoked and exchanged—and I walk out of that sermon changed, opened, and renewed, for you have shone the light of the Bible into the depths of my soul.
—*Charles Denison*

Now it's time to get even more specific advice in response to our question, "What are we supposed to be attentive to?" Creative writers advise us to cultivate our knack for noticing the people, events, and places we encounter in our daily lives. To put it in a novelist's terms, we need to develop our knack for noticing character, plot, scene, and imagery. If you want a way to remember them, make them all start with "S": sheroes/heroes, story line, scene, and sensation. Our focus in the rest of this chapter is on developing our knack for noticing character and plot.

Knack for Noticing Desire

A number of authors agree that the essence of character in fiction is desire, or, as Robert Olen Butler puts it, yearning:

> The characters who stand up and make us care are so in love that they are willing to risk their reputations and their souls (Anna Karenina), or so committed to a cause that they will devote their lives to it (Robin Hood, among many), or driven by a passion to know (Faust) or to get revenge (Hamlet) or to solve the mystery, climb the mountain, uncover the past, find out who they really are. . . . This quality of yearning or determination is what makes us catch our breath, hope for the best, [and] fear the worst.[15]

If desire is the core of character out of which plot grows, let's take a page out of the fiction writer's book. What he does is peruse his own inward life and that of those around him in the service of creating fictional characters. To do that, he has to practice empathy with others, being attuned to what he perceives to be their desires.

The lesson for preachers is that we need to practice our knack for noticing desire. We need to start with our own, since desire is the core of our character out of which the plot of our life is growing. Attentiveness to one's own character, one's own desires and yearnings, is an essential starting place and recurring touchstone for the fiction writer. One creative writing teacher has students describe their characters in a fill-in-the-blanks exercise.

<u>Name of character</u> is a ____-year-old man/woman who wants
_____.[16]

Example: John is a suspicious thirty-year-old man who wants respect.

When studying a text, try writing such a sentence, first about yourself, and then about the people in the text. For example, the man at the pool of Bethzatha (John 5) is an exhausted fifty-year-old man who wants a miracle.

John Gardner liked to tell the story of the time he did a reading and a woman approached him and said, "You know, I think I like your stories, but I'm not sure I like you." He did not hesitate before he replied, "That's all right. I'm a better person when I write." "No matter how pigheaded, stupid or imperfect a writer might be in his personal life (and certainly the stories of how badly many outstanding writers have lied are legion) what he did on the pages offered an opportunity . . . to speak with clarity and precision, work in a spirit of love and compassion, and revise his thoughts and feelings to the point where they could be most helpful and do no harm."[17]

I don't have to tell you that the roles of preacher and novelist are different. While preachers don't become preachers so they can be liked, it's a warning sign if we feel we are presenting ourselves as a different, better character in our public preaching than we do in our private lives. In being attentive to character and the desire that fuels it, we need to start with and keep after our own. Thoreau said it well when he said we need to "know our own bone." "Pursue, keep up with, circle round and round your life. . . . Know your own bone: gnaw at it, bury it, unearth it, and gnaw at it still."[18] If yearning is the essence of character and the genesis of plot, we need to stay attentive to our yearnings and be honest with ourselves about just what we yearn for most. Periodic adjustments may be necessary.

John Gardner said there are two kinds of close observation and accuracy that are crucial for a fiction writer. One is the ability to see clearly and document well one's own feelings, experiences, and prejudices. The second turns this clarity on others. The novelist also needs to be able to report with convincing precision how the world looks "to a child, a young woman, an elderly murderer, or the governor of Utah." The writer's gift is for rendering the precise observations and feelings of a wide variety of characters. Therefore, cultivate the gift for inhabiting other lives.[19]

Novelist Antonya Nelson takes Gardner's advice to literal lengths. She says, "I've witnessed an autopsy and climbed in the Absaroka Mountains. Whatever my characters remember or experience, I too must understand."[20] What if we preachers applied this to our parishioners? It might not involve witnessing autopsies and climbing in the Absaroka Mountains, but it might. It certainly would involve knowing about and experiencing our people's workday worlds.

Gardner believed that the best novelists were those who were not judgmental of others. The novelist "cannot love some of his characters and despise others."[21] Gardner believed that a writer needed to see each of his characters from the inside, as someone as real and complex as we are ourselves. The writer must not only be capable of understanding people different from himself, but be fascinated by such people. He must have sufficient self-esteem that he is not threatened by difference, sufficient warmth and sympathy, and a sufficient concern with fairness that he wants to value people different from himself; he must also have a sufficient faith in the goodness of life that he can not only tolerate but celebrate a world of differences, conflicts, and oppositions.[22]

Knack for Noticing Choices

Look around you at the qualities and actions of people. Character is revealed in everyday, small matters, of course—small deeds of cruelty or kindness. But character is seen most clearly when there are crucial choices that break or make a character. The make-or-break decision is the genesis of plot. Make a habit of looking around you at the qualities and actions of people you know of and people you know.

A pastor is caught planning an Internet rendezvous with a police officer posing as a thirteen-year-old girl. A basketball coach, fresh from being fired, wishes his successor well at a press conference. A police officer on a routine traffic stop pushes three people out of the path of an oncoming car and is hurt himself. We are in the habit of letting such events glide by, good and bad, either shaking our heads ("That's too bad") or nodding our heads ("Isn't that great!"). But we need to get in the habit of labeling such events as "character-revealing crossroads."

When we get in the habit of paying attention to these crossroads in the lives of others, we start paying closer attention to our own. Why did I respond negatively to constructive criticism? Why, despite my commitment to a more sane schedule, did I say yes without hesitation to the invitation to preach when my clergy colleague called this morning? We have a thousand choices a day, mini-crossroads that test and reveal our character. Attentiveness to character in those around us hones our observation of what is going on within us.

Knack for Noticing Interactions between People

Another place to look for character is in the interactions of one person with another. It is easy to have a noble character when we are alone. What happens in our lives, in the lives of biblical characters, when we and they interact with others, often in conflictual situations? What qualities of character reveal themselves then?

New insights into biblical characters may surface when we observe their interactions. The two priests walked by. The Samaritan stopped. Why? David gave into lust and greed. Why? Esau, who earlier had vowed to kill his brother Jacob, forgave him for his conniving and betrayal. I'm not sure I would have. What events and insights went into that reversal?

Knack for Noticing What Sticks Out

Fiction writer and novelist Josip Evanovitch points out that not all characters in fiction undergo a crucial change. Sometimes their stability in the face of pressure is a virtue. Job's refusal to admit to sin in the face of his friends' accusations is one such example. The women's faithfulness to Jesus, standing at the cross, is an example of unflinching loyalty. At other times unchangeability is a growth-inhibiting rigidity. Still, a crisis is what shines a light on character. Says Evanovitch, "Whether or not there's a change in you, character is not the part of you that conforms, but rather, that sticks out." So a caricaturist seeks out oddities in a face: big jaws, slanted foreheads, strong creases. The part of the character that does not conform builds a conflict, and the conflict makes the story. Find something conflicting in a character, some trait sticking out of the plane, that creates dimension and complexity.[23] Practice this as you search yourself, the people you know, and the people you hear and read about.

Traditional Korean folktales and stories are rich resources that can illuminate biblical texts and illustrate sermons. . . . If we want to make sermons practical to the lives of common people, we can find an important place for aphorisms or proverbs in sermon preparation.
—Jung Young Lee

Knack for Noticing Round Characters

British novelist E. M. Forster (1879–1970), in his treatise *Aspects of the Novel* (1927), first made the now-famous distinction between "flat" characters and "round" characters. He shared Virginia Woolf's concept of character as something in perpetual flux, illuminated differently by different moments of experience.[24] A flat character has few traits, and all are predictable. The absent-minded professor. The prim librarian. The shallow socialite. They are caricatures. Round characters have three dimensions. They are complex, possessing conflicting traits, both positive and negative. She is paranoid, but thoughtful. He is demanding, yet forgiving. She is highly critical of others, yet generous with her money.

In C. W. Smith's novel *Purple Hearts*, for example—set in a small town in Texas during World War II—one of the main characters, Sylvia, is prone to self-pity and vanity. She sleeps with another man while her husband is away in the army. Yet one evening, on her way home from work, she passes a black solider, his wife, and infant son sitting on a bench at the train station. They are haggard and exhausted. She invites them to spend the night in her spare room. Why? Because she lacks racial prejudice and is empathetic. And because she knows how much it will annoy her mother-in-law. She's a round character.

All of this is to imprint in our minds that one of the key things creative writers counsel us to notice is character. Practice being observant of the people around you. Record your impressions in a notebook or journal. But don't be like the nineteenth-century novelist Anthony Trollope, who went to parties and spent the whole time staring, first at one person, then another, for ten minutes each, hardly answering when people addressed him. That would just be creepy.[25]

Knack for Noticing Plots

Creative writers advise us to be attentive to plots. We can pay attention to the plots around us, within us, and within and around the biblical text. Plot essentially answers the reporter's questions, "What?" "How?" and "Why?"

Southern writer Eudora Welty tells of growing up in Jackson, Mississippi. Her mother didn't enjoy talking on the phone but had friends who did. Eudora would sit on the stairs and listen to her mother's half of the conversation. One caller was quite a talker. Eudora remembers her mother replying, now and then, "Well, I declare," or "You don't say so," or "Surely not."

> When she hung up I would ask "What did she say?"
> "She wasn't *saying* a thing in this world," sighed my mother. "She was just ready to talk, that's all."[26]

Says Welty, "Long before I wrote stories, I listened for stories. Listening for them is something more acute than listening to them. . . . It's an early form of participation in what goes on. Listening children know stories are there. When their elders sit and begin, children are just waiting and hoping for one to come out, like a mouse from its hole."[27]

In her memoir *One Writer's Beginnings,* Welty gives glimpses of how her habit of listening for stories shaped her fiction. Her use of weather to indicate mood was sparked by her father's preoccupation with meteorology and her love of stories by her mother's friends who loved to tell neighborhood stories.

Her tendency to put parades into her work comes from the year someone convinced the circus parade to march up a different street from the usual way to the Fairgrounds, to go past the house of a little boy whose illness kept him in bed. "He was carried to the window to watch it go by. Just for him the ponderous elephants, the plumes, the spangles, the acrobats, the clowns, the caged lion, the band playing, the steam calliope, the whole thing!"[28]

The frequency of schoolteacher characters in her fiction came from Miss Duling, the stern but endearing principal of the Davis School across from her house. Her appreciation for humor was nurtured in the town movie house where she and her brother Edward collapsed in laughter at the "antic pantomime of the silent screen," Buster Keaton, Charlie Chaplin, Ben Blue and the Keystone Kops.[29]

Everywhere you go simply say to yourself, "There is a story in this." Unless we consciously remind ourselves that what we are experiencing is a story, it will slip downstream past us. Like a person with a camera looking for a good picture, you will start to see the stories around you.
—Paul Scott Wilson

Ernest Gaines, best known as the author of *The Autobiography of Miss Jane Pitman,* was born in 1933 and raised on a plantation near False River in central Louisiana. He used to write letters for the older people who didn't have the education to write their own. He said, "I had to listen carefully to what they had to say and how they said it, the words they tried to use. I put their stories down on paper, and they would give me teacakes." Gaines later attended Stanford University as a Wallace Stegner fellow. He says he became a writer when he sat in the college library and began reading a lot. "I began to read many great novels and stories and I did not see myself or my people in any of them. It was then that I tried to write." It took leaving the plantation to realize that those stories should be told.[30]

Willa Cather once said, "There are only two or three human stories, and they go on repeating themselves as fiercely as if they had never happened before."[31] Ron Tobias, in his book *20 Master Plots: And How to*

Build Them, not surprisingly, lists twenty master plots. They are quest, adventure, pursuit, rescue, escape, revenge, the riddle, rivalry, underdog, temptation, metamorphosis, transformation, maturation, forbidden love, sacrifice, discovery, wretched excess, ascension, and descension.

In each of these plots, there are three acts. Act 1 is the setup. Act 2 is the complication. Act 3 is the resolution. The three-act plot is a standard dramatic structure often used, with variations, in novels and screenwriting. Tobias describes several features common to all twenty plots. One is that tension fuels each plot. A second is that opposition creates tension. The third is that tension grows as opposition increases. A fourth is that change is the point of the plot. A fifth is that the central character performs the central action of the climax of the plot.[32]

> *Weaving is an image not simply of actuality but of possibility. . . . This image has at its heart the interlacing of conflict and struggle with vision and hope. . . . The weaving metaphor proclaims that the preacher and her environment are an interwoven fabric in which every strand crosses every other.*
> —Christine M. Smith

Our sermons don't always follow a single protagonist on a quest; nor do they always proceed from complication to resolution. But they involve, in some way, tension, opposition, and change. Hone your knack for noticing these three dynamics. Where do you see them happening in your family, your circle of friends and acquaintances, your church, your community, and beyond? How about in text and the world behind the text? The creative writer engages in this plot fieldwork, this close observation of the seeds of story lines, to create fictional worlds and stories. The preacher does so to depict an alternative world: a vision of how daily life would look if we lived it as God desires that we live (the kingdom of God). Remember that you don't have to know exactly how your observations will figure into a future sermon. Add them to that compost heap we talked about and see what happens.

William Faulkner accounted for his work by simply stating he liked to listen. "I don't go out with a notebook, but I like these people, that is, I like to listen to them, the way they talk or the things they talk about. . . . I would go around with [my uncle] and sit on the front galleries of country stores and listen to the talk."[33] Faulkner may not have gone around with a notebook, but he was William Faulkner. You and I need to go around with a notebook.

It's time for us to get up out of our rocking chairs and stretch. Walk around the porch. Refill our plates and cups. If everyone is back now, let's recap and move ahead.

Chapter Three

Noticing How?

Habits for Heightened Attentiveness

We said when we first sat down on the porch that the three obstacles to cultivating imagination were lack of discipline, lack of daring, and lack of direction. If our obstacle is lack of daring, we need to pray daily for courage. If our obstacle is lack of direction, I hope the advice from these authors has sharpened your knack for noticing, your sense of what you need to be attentive to in the inscape, landscape, and textscape of your daily life. If our obstacle is lack of discipline, here are several prescriptions.

Carry a Small Notebook (or the Electronic Equivalent), and Don't Let Anything Get Away

Annie Dillard said it succinctly: "To find a honey tree, first catch a bee."[1] To catch your bees, commit to carrying a low-tech pocket-size notebook and pen, or the appropriate electronic device. Record insights and preserve them; capture them as they arise.

Eudora Welty, in her memoir *One Writer's Beginnings*, describes her first full-time job as a junior publicity agent for the Works Progress Administration in the 1930s. She traveled around her home state of Mississippi taking pictures and gathering information. She says she learned about writing by taking pictures. "I learned in the doing how ready I had to be.

[Meditation is] a spiritual process of cultivating the vast potential of the mind beyond the limitations imposed by internal and external human circumstances.
—Eun Joo Kim

Life doesn't hold still. A good snapshot stopped a moment from running away. Photography taught me that to be able to capture transience, by being ready to click the shutter at the crucial moment, was the greatest need I had."[2]

Keep a Journal

In addition to a portable notebook, you need an at-home journal. Many novelists recommend journal keeping as a means of exercising and enhancing one's powers of observation. Novelist and creative writing coach Janet Burroway explained, "If we know at dawn that we will write in our journals, we will half-consciously tell the story of our day to ourselves as we live it, finding a phrase to catch whatever catches our eye. Whatever invites our attention or sympathy, our anger or curiosity, may be the beginning of a character, a story theme."[3] For the preacher, it may begin to shape and, later, to show up in a sermon.

Burroway makes it clear that the journal isn't a diary, though you can certainly record your feelings and problems. You need to make it more outer-directed than a diary. You are training yourself to observe the outside world. She suggests we make a habit of recording something we experience or notice each day. It might be something we overhear, an unexpected event, an unusual person, a news story, or a new fact we learned in a class. Whatever it is, knowing we are going to write every day instills in us the habit of paying attention to life with writing in mind. The writer experiences the world with all five senses with an eye and ear toward what use he can make of it. When we write, we need to tell our inner critic to hush and give ourselves permission to write freely.[4]

[We need to] make the innocent eye the alerted eye, the eye that probes and detects the shadowed depths of our mythological worlds and is aware of its own distortions and blind spots.
—Thomas Troeger

Novelist Gail Godwin says that "a journal is a dialogue with the self, and then it becomes a dialogue with the selves. It's a way to keep track of where you've been and who you were, it's a way to keep yourself honest. It can also be a form of prayer. Prayer is a way of conversing with an other, an other that's not you, not God in myself but an Other. The journal can be that too."[5]

An expanded form of the journal is what we might call "the Preacher's Notebook," modeled on "the Writer's Notebook." Novelist and creative-writing teacher Charles Johnson keeps a writer's notebook in which he records ideas and character sketches, and in which he places articles he has cut out of magazines or newspapers or printed from the Web. He says that periodically he goes through the clippings and the reflections to see if there is a thought that can be useful in the story or novel he is writing. It is a memory aid, helping him recall thoughts and feelings.[6]

Write Morning Pages

For the past couple of years I've been practicing what creative writers call "freewriting." Creativity expert and author Julia Cameron has baptized these "morning pages." They are the literary equivalent of scales at the piano or a short gym workout. You move your pen across the page for twenty minutes or three pages, whichever comes first. Don't censor; just keep the pen moving. The morning pages, says Cameron, are "a Western form of mediation, because most of us hate sitting there. . . . You get up in the morning . . . and write three pages of longhand writing about anything. . . . It's stream of consciousness, or . . . 'stream of gripe.' Stream of worry. Stream of preoccupation."[7]

Natalie Goldberg, a practitioner of freewriting, compares it to Zen meditation or "quiet sitting." In meditation,

> The object is to let go of thoughts and anchor the mind with the breath in the present moment. . . . Thoughts are sticky and they keep coming back. In writing practice you grab the thoughts and write them down, and by writing them down, you go on to the next one and you keep moving through them. You are anchoring your mind with your pen. Your thoughts become a quick stream you're sitting in. So they're not quite as sticky. Writing practice is a way of settling into a quiet place. I get to run through the thoughts and then let them go.[8]

A subcategory of freewriting is called "focused freewriting." Pick a topic and focus on it. Write for five or ten minutes saying anything at all about it—*anything at all*—in any order. Choose a topic that is troubling you or that you wonder about. Say, "dealing with difficult people," or "things I wish I could say in my sermons but probably won't ever say." If you are preaching on a particular text, choose an image or word or idea from it and freewrite about it.

Focused Freewriting: "What If?"

Start with the question, "What if?" Finish the question and then free associate around it. Absolutely anything that pops into your head is fair game.

Ideas, situations, connections, images—no matter how bizarre. This is a problem-solving technique, but it also generates energy for imaginative writing. The preacher can apply this to scriptural text. What if there had only been eight commandments? What would you leave out? What if it wasn't God who caused the flood? What if Jesus, rather than praying, "If you are willing, remove this cup from me; yet, not my will but yours be done" (Luke 22:42), had said to God, "No way I'm taking this cup," and headed for the hills?

The imaginative process in preaching is like the art of sailing a boat. "We cannot make the wind blow; we cannot compel the Holy Spirit to fill our imaginations with wind and fire. But we can trim the sails and tend the helm. We can practice those disciplines of prayer and thought that open us to God's revelation."
—Thomas Troeger[9]

We can apply this to our lives. "What if we really lived by this text?" "What if *I* took the first step toward mending this relationship?" "What if *I* summoned the courage to do what I dread?"

Listen to Music

A number of novelists talk about the importance of music in sparking their creative process, among them Steve Katz and Raymond Federman, both devotees of jazz.[10] Robert Olen Butler says he "always writes to music, usually classical or jazz, almost always without words."[11]

The power of radio, with its ability to engage the imagination of the listener by "permitting" the creation of "our own image in the mind's eye," is an important reminder to those who see the electronic visual media as entirely dominant. . . . Having the space to draw their own images liberates listeners to participate or interact with what they are hearing. . . . This understanding of the creative and derivative powers of the imagination further shows how important it is for broadcasters and preachers to engage their listener's inner eye or visual imagination.[12]

Read

Novelists and teachers of creative writing recommend that aspiring literary artists read widely from fiction and also from nonfiction to hone their language skills and to expand the world of their experience. Read poetry, essays, short stories, and novels. Read editorials, news magazines, and creative nonfiction. Reading the language of gifted language users keeps the language pump primed.

Says novelist Antonya Nelson, "Reading makes you accustomed to inhabiting others' lives and sensibilities. . . . Inhabiting the life of a

Cultivate your imagination's ability both to criticize and to energize.
—Walter Brueggemann

person who is different from you in every single way is a challenging, broadening experience."[13]

Walk

Walking is an overlooked tool of creativity. Says Julia Cameron, "It is often on walks that you will integrate a problem, or if you have a tangled plot line as a writer, you'll suddenly see a new solution. When you walk, you are able to hear more cleanly and more keenly."[14]

The irreplaceable elements in proclamation preparation are the rests. . . . The transition following a rest may result in key changes, tempo augmentation, or volume modification. In singing it is a time to gather one's energy or emotion. . . . [Rests are] those places where preachers hear from God. They allow us to remain in tune by following God's direction.
—Teresa L. Fry Brown

The Artist's Date

The "artist's date" is a term coined by Julia Cameron. She recommends that, once a week, you go out and do something "festive and pre-planned." By "festive," she means something you enjoy doing, something that may have no apparent, immediate payoff. It is a date with yourself and with your own creative consciousness. Do not take children or spouses, and do something interesting and expansive for yourself. Says Cameron, "Art is an image-using system, so in order to draw from that well, we have to consciously keep that ecosystem stocked. What you do with artist dates is you turn the dial so that you are

[Play is] when you let the fields lie fallow, and they surprise you with a profusion of wildflowers. . . . It's where the unexpected comes to life.
—Raewynne Whiteley

on receive. You let images in." The morning pages are a way of figuring out where you are, signaling to yourself where you need help. The artist's dates are a way of receiving sustenance.[15]

The sun is setting in hues of orange and pink, and it's time to call it a day. Thank you for taking time out from your busy schedule to listen to the advice of these writers living and dead for cultivating our imaginations, honing our KFN through notebooks, journals, walking, music, and artist's dates.

By now I suspect you are eager to go check your voicemail, text messages, and e-mail. None of us can stay on the porch forever. Being presented with such an array of strategies for cultivating our imagination might leave us feeling overwhelmed and frustrated because we know we can't practice all of them all the time. In response, we could caricature these suggestions and laugh together about how artsy they sound. Better yet, let's grab onto them like a lifeline thrown to a drowning person, and figure out how we can work at least a couple of them into our daily lives.

As a preacher, you have been given beautiful feet.
Use them. Slow down. Don't race through life; walk.
When we are walking, we are able to stop and notice
a lovely flower that is blooming beside us. We are able
to appreciate the people around us. We have more of a
chance of seeing God's footprints that surround us. The
Scriptures will always be our most important resource.
But where else might we look for God's footprints?
—Lucy Lind Hogan

Part 2

Shaping the Sermon

Chapter Four

Sermon Shapes

Fiction Writing Strategies for Sermons

You are in your study at your desk with your Bible, commentaries, and legal pads spread out in front of you. Imagination is in the corner in its bathrobe, drinking tea, offering moral support. But it's going to take more than just being in the same room with imagination. We need to know how to use its insights to shape the sermon manuscript we have to produce this week. If only a group of creative writers could come to us and offer us some fiction writing principles to guide us. In the realm of imagination, anything can happen . . . so lo and behold, here they are, lining up at the door.

In this chapter, I'm asking you to imagine yourself struggling, as I do from week to week, with various sermon pitfalls. As we struggle, various fiction writers enter our study space to stand over our shoulder and offer fiction writing principles that address our particular problem. We don't have to be working on a text that is itself a story to utilize their advice. We don't have to commit to shaping every sermon according to the classic three-part dramatic structure of conflict, crisis, and resolution. Fiction writers' imaginative strategies can help us engage listeners' emotions while informing their minds in any sermon.

The seven aspects of the fiction writer's craft are sheroes and heroes (character), story line (plot), sequence (form), sensation (imagery and sensory detail), scene, setting, and sightline (point of view). This chapter offers advice with regard to several of these categories for our sermon struggles. It provides, not a panacea, but some fresh perspectives.

What follows is a typology of four types of sermon struggles. I realize that this presentation is much more clear-cut than the blurry reality it oversimplifies. Individual sermons can fit more than one, none, or all of the categories. They are as follows:

- The sermon that is *coherent and entertaining but lacks depth* (congregational symptom: *malnutrition*)
- The sermon that *tries to teach, but is incoherent* (hard to follow) (congregational symptom: *mental confusion*)
- The sermon that is *coherent but boring* (congregational symptoms: *general loss of interest and pleasure; numbness or lack of sensation*)
- The sermon that, while it may be interesting and teaches people something, *offers false teaching* (congregational symptoms: *mood swings between false optimism and false guilt*)

The Sermon That Is Coherent and Entertaining but Lacks Depth

I don't think any of us ever embarks intentionally on a ministry of "preaching lite." None of us purposely, week after week, offers sermons intended only to entertain, without concern for teaching our people the knowledge and wisdom that come from plumbing the depths of life and Scripture. But lite preaching happens to just about all of us some of the time.

Maybe it happens this way: We are pressed for time. We go to the text, and we discern an obvious theme. Perhaps, in preaching on Psalm 121, we quickly decide to preach on "God helps us in times of trouble." That does seem to be the obvious theme of the psalm. We offer four or five examples of God helping people in times of trouble. Never mind that lifting up our "eyes to the hills" (v. 1) may refer to the fact that that's where the robbers and ambushers hid to swoop down on travelers below. Never mind that the experience of many in my congregation belies an easy assurance that God "[keeps us] from all evil" (v. 7). Nobody will be able to accuse the sermon of not having a theme that ties it together, but neither will they experience it addressing the depth of Israel's faith as expressed in the Psalter as it intersects with our lives today. The excuse that we are trying to appeal to people who are new to the faith is just that, an excuse. The long-term effect on a congregation of a steady diet of shallow sermons is malnutrition. Vital nutrients are habitually missing from our sermonic diet.

By describing a sermon as lacking in depth, I mean it is a sermon that fails to be attentive to key aspects of congregational context or text. For example, suppose I'm preaching on Exodus 15 and I ignore verses 4 and 5, where the pharaoh's soldiers and chariots "went down into the depths like a stone." I would think that it would be important to tag that as morally troubling, to point out that their lives have value as well as those of the Israelites, and to raise the question, "What we are to make of a God who champions one people at the expense of another?"

Suppose I'm preaching on Proverbs 16:17, which assures us, "The highway of the upright avoids evil; those who guard their way preserve their lives." I would want to acknowledge that the experiences of many in the congregation contradict that promise: illness, deaths of loved ones, experiences of injustice. A preacher's obliviousness to the realities of his listeners' daily experience is a key characteristic of the shallow sermon. I need to dig into the meanings of key words in the context of the book of Proverbs to pull the nuance out of what seems to be the surface meaning. I need to put this saying in conversation with others that affirm it or contest it, from both the Old and New Testaments.

Advice from Fiction Writers to Add Depth to Your Sermon

Choose a Subject Worthy of Your Audience

Novelist Edith Wharton urges would-be novelists to choose a subject worthy of their audience.[1] Wharton believes that "the literary artist seeks by instinct those subjects in which some phase of our common plight stands forth dramatically . . . in which there is a kind of summary of life's . . . occurrences."[2]

"There are subjects trivial in appearance, and subjects trivial to the core; and the novelist ought to be able to discern at a glance between the two . . ." The novelist "learns . . . to resist surface-attractions, and probe his story to the depths before he begins to tell it."[3]

In my view, a sermon dedicated to proving the identity of Jacob's adversary at Peniel in Genesis 32 is not worthy of my audience. It is not of sufficient import. What is a worthy theme, however, is that God sticks with us in our struggles, whomever our adversary may be, and offers us a changed identity and purpose as a result of the struggle.

In preaching on any or all of the "lost and found" parables of Luke 15 (lost sheep, lost coin, lost son), focusing exclusively on repentance as waiting for God to find us is not a theme worthy of my audience. It is a partial truth and not the only posture of the life of faith commended by the parables of Luke 15 in the larger context of his entire Gospel.

Pay Attention to Character

In the opening chapter of *Literature: Structure, Sound and Sense*, the authors distinguish between escape literature and interpretive literature:

> Escape literature is written purely for entertainment—to help us pass the time agreeably. Interpretive literature is written to broaden and deepen and sharpen our awareness of life. Escape literature takes us away from the real world: it enables us temporarily to forget our troubles. Interpretive literature takes us, through the imagination, deeper *into* the real world: it enables us to understand our troubles. Escape literature has as its only object pleasure. Interpretive literature has as its object pleasure *plus* understanding.[4]

People, including myself, like lite fiction, in which the protagonist is a stereotype: a plucky, gorgeous romance heroine; a gritty, disillusioned ex-cop, and so on. Such literature sells because it has an exciting plot with lots of action, as well as the assurance that the protagonist will not die at the end and will also get what he or she wanted from the beginning. The protagonist doesn't necessarily change between the beginning and the ending, but the events do. It is escape reading, and we don't expect the author's arm to reach out from the pages and pull us into a transformative journey in which our values are questioned and replaced with deeper ones by the end.

An author of interpretive fiction would ask a preacher this: have you constructed your sermon with the aim that, by the end of it, your listeners have been changed and not just escaped?

Predictable plots, intact protagonists, and happy endings are fine for lite fiction, but more troubling for lite preaching. Lite preaching can take lots of forms. We can tell people good news without showing them when, where, and how it can be true in their daily lives. We can tell people jokes and stories for their own sake. We can tell people what we think they want to hear as if it were true. Lite sermons are the result of lack of attentiveness, and we know from chapter 2 that two obstacles to attentiveness are lack of discipline and lack of daring.

The authors of *Literature: An Introduction to Reading and Writing* eloquently summarize the purpose of literature, attributing to it several character-shaping functions.

> Literature helps us grow, both personally and intellectually.
>
> It enables us to recognize human dreams and struggles in different places and times that we would never otherwise know.

It provides the comparative basis from which we can see worthiness in the aims of all people, and it therefore helps us see beauty in the world around us.

It exercises our emotions, through interest, concern, tension, excitement, hope, fear, regret, laughter, and sympathy.

It shapes goals and values by clarifying our own identities, both positively, through acceptance of the admirable in human beings, and negatively, through rejection of the sinister.

It helps us shape our judgments through the comparisons of the good and the bad.

It makes us human.[5]

Lite fiction doesn't aspire to these goals. Lite preaching doesn't accomplish them.

Pay Attention to Imagery

Superficial sermons often result when we mine the text quickly for an idea and then extrapolate it and string stories onto it like clothes hung out to dry on a clothesline. Fiction writers would encourage us to be attentive to the sensory world of the text and to any images that it holds. Once you start asking yourself about the significance of an image in context, your sermon begins to have potential, not only for clarity, but also for a depth encounter between text and life.

For example, suppose you are preaching on Matthew's parable of the Ten Bridesmaids (Matt. 25:1–13). They let their lamps go out. So what? Except that light is a symbol in Matthew's Gospel for discipleship and faithfulness to Christ (Matt. 5:14–16).

Suppose you are preaching on Luke's parable of the Friend at Midnight (Luke 11:5–8), which features someone standing on the doorstep seeking bread. If we're in a hurry, we might ignore the metaphor or spiritualize it. If we slow down and go deeper, we'll notice that bread is a pervasive, profound metaphor for sustenance throughout the entire Bible: manna in the wilderness (Exod. 16), "not by bread alone" (Matt. 4:4; Luke 4:4), and bread from heaven (John 6:22–59). We'll ask ourselves about bread's significance in the Gospel of Luke, in the lives of our congregation, in our own lives.

Pay Attention to Setting

Superficial sermons can also result from the preacher's lack of attention to setting. Actually, we need to attend to two settings. One is the setting in which members of the congregation conduct their daily lives. A second is the setting in which members of the original audience of the biblical text conducted their daily lives.

Novelists know that setting is crucial because character grows out of setting. That's not just true in fiction. Our characters grow by responding to the people, places, and events of our unique settings. As our characters grow and change, we influence the people, places, and events of our unique setting.

If your sermons are sometimes a superficial idea strung with anecdotes, concluding with "The moral of the story is," try thinking like a novelist. Think and feel and study your way into the setting. It may be the decadence of the city of Corinth. It may be the nasty squabble between Jews and Gentiles that lies beneath the surface of Matthew's Gospel. It may be the turmoil of the postexilic community, struggling with the question "Why are we suffering?" that pulses through the pages of Job. Whatever it is, you need to allow it to come alive for your listeners. Our characters depend on it.

Science-fiction writer and creative-writing teacher Nancy Kress reminds writers to remember when they are creating their character(s) that character grows out of setting. An author needs to have thought in detail about the setting for her story. It needs to exist "complete in the mind of the author, with not only physical features but also prevailing values, beliefs, class structure, economics and social customs. To do you any good as a generator of incidents, a setting must be as complex as real-life settings are."[6]

Kress calls on writers to understand their settings not just physically, but sociologically and economically as well. "Fiction is not sociology. But fiction, like sociology, is about human behavior." The author needs to have thought about the values and expectations of the setting so that he can portray how his characters are at odds with some aspect of their setting, or how it affects their strengths, weaknesses, and desires.[7]

Of course, the preacher can't always know as much as she'd like about the setting of a biblical text. But generally a sermon gains depth when the preacher reflects as fully as possible on the impact of the setting of the biblical text on its audience then and now.

The Sermon That Tries to Teach, but Is Incoherent

I spend a lot of time as a teacher of preaching trying to help preachers clarify the flow of their thought. Screenwriters call this the "throughline."

The throughline is the plotline that answers the question, "What happens to the protagonist?"[8] In a sermon it's called the focus or the theme. It's what the sermon is about, summed up in one sentence. Novelists differ in the way they work, but many say they figure out the last scene of their novel first and then plot the whole novel toward it. The traditional, deductive, three-point sermon states its throughline (its focus) first. Preachers who favor inductive preaching (moving from the specifics to the general) work more like fiction writers; their sermons cut the focus from its spot as the first sentence of the sermon and paste it in as the last sentence of the manuscript. Everything in the sermon flows toward it.

When I edit students' sermons, I write things in the margins in green (not red) pen like, "Why are you telling me this? Why are you telling me this now? How does this relate to what has gone before?" "How does it pave the way for what comes next?" I'm articulating the questions our listeners unconsciously apply to our sermons as we speak them. A steady diet of incoherent sermons, sermons with tangled-up throughlines, leaves the congregation in a state of mental confusion. There are several possible causes of the incoherent sermon.

It could be that you are tired and emotionally scattered. Get some rest.

It may be that you have too many themes competing for your attention. The answer to the question, "How many points should a sermon have?" is "At least one." But you can have too much of a good thing. Pick the theme you can preach with the most excitement, and promise the others you'll include them in another sermon on another day.

Some fiction writers recommend an exercise called "clustering" to help you organize your thoughts when you have too many ideas vying to be the lead theme for your sermon. Pick a word that represents your central subject, and write it in the center of the page. Circle it. For two or three minutes, free associate by jotting down around it any word, image, action, emotion, or part of speech that comes to mind. Every now and again, circle the words you have written and draw lines or arrows between words that seem to connect. Keep going. Don't worry about making sense. Take a few seconds to look at what you've done. Then start writing.[9]

Your sermon may lack coherence because you lack desire. Let's think like a novelist about this problem of incoherence, the sermon whose throughline meanders, or is scattered, disjointed, or in pieces. A fiction writer might suggest that the problem is that you, as the protagonist of your own sermon, are suffering from a lack of desire.

Janet Burroway tells us that "to engage our attention and sympathy, the protagonist in a novel must want something and want it intensely. A common fault in novice writers is that they create a main character who is essentially passive."[10] Could that be you in approaching your sermon preparation? I've been there. I'm not talking about times when I'm waiting faithfully for God's word. I'm talking about times when, for various reasons, I don't feel like preparing a sermon. My heart's not in it. I don't really want anything intensely except not to have to do it.

Robert Olen Butler insists, "Fiction is the art of human yearning. . . . Absolutely essential to any work of fictional narrative art [is] a character who yearns. And that is not the same as a character who simply has problems. . . . The yearning is also the thing that generates what we call plot, because the elements of the plot come from thwarted or blocked or challenged attempts to fulfill that yearning."[11]

I'll admit it. I am a character who has problems, but do I also yearn? Of course, it's not all about me. God is the protagonist of every sermon. The theological question we too often forget to ask is, "What is the character of God according to this text? And what does God want?" That can sometimes be a troubling or challenging question to ask. It may call for a conference call between the text at hand and other canonical voices. The other question is, "What do my people want and need?" Those questions of divine and congregational desire can help bring coherence to a sermon that is scattered and disjointed.

But coming back to you for a moment. If your sermon is incoherent, it may be because you don't have a high enough stake in it, or you haven't allowed yourself to be addressed at your depths by the challenge and the good news that God is trying to convey to you through the text. You are not in touch with the one, intense, unifying desire that you yearn to have fulfilled by the end of the sermon. This isn't the place to examine all the reasons that might be, but it might be. The reason my sermon is incoherent, scattered, in pieces, and disjointed may be because I am.

Elizabeth McCracken, author of *The Giant's House*, quotes her writing teacher Allan Gurganus on passion in writing. "Allan always said that in order to move your readers, to put them through any kind of emotional state, you have to put yourself through ten times that much for it to translate to the page. That's the physics of writing. If you're a good writer, you intensely feel anything you write."[12]

If you are afraid your sermon is incoherent, try applying the "physics of writing" to your manuscript. Consider the following character questions checklist:

1. What is your character as the preacher? What is the desire that drives your life?
2. Is God a character in the sermon? What is God's character—that is to say, what is God's desire?
3. Do you have a clear sense of how you hope the sermon will shape the character of listeners (influence their desires)?
4. How are you hoping listeners' character will change as a result of entering into the sermon?

Fiction Writers' Advice for the Incoherent Sermon

Enlist a Guiding Image or Metaphor to Organize and Unify the Sermon

Ask yourself if an image in the sermon wants to be moved from the body of the sermon to the introduction, to become the guiding, unifying image of the sermon. See if an image has arisen in your thinking, either from the text or everyday life, that would qualify as a guiding image for the sermon that you introduce at the outset. This often happens, fiction writers say. They discover, three-quarters of the way through a novel, that a metaphor, image, or theme keeps tapping them on the shoulder; they then rewrite the whole work, threading the image through to make it more prominent.

In my Palm Sunday sermon in chapter 6, "Silent Disciples, Shouting Stones," the shouting stones became the guiding metaphor in a sermon that took the shape of a series of scenes, each featuring a nondisciple who was loyal to Jesus in ways that the disciples were not.

In "My Favorite Angel" (Matt. 28:1–10) in chapter 6, the abruptness of the angel's message and the focus of his mission made me think of a UPS driver who is not on your porch to chat, but to offer you something important that it's up to you to open and use.

Check the Sequence of Your Scenes

F. A. Rockwell reminds fiction writers that the difference between a published story and a rejected story is that the former has better plot organization and includes scenes that give the story a colorful, pictorial quality.[13] In our sermons, we often state a main idea and find brief stories to illustrate it. Rockwell would tell us, instead, to think of our sermon as having a plot and to break it down into scenes. A scene is a single situation, dialogue, or episode in a narrative or drama.[14] We preachers tend to think of the segments of our sermons as points in an outline, though we'll see in chapter 5 some newer options such as "moves" (David

Buttrick), "episodes" (Mike Graves), and "pages" (Paul Scott Wilson). Try thinking about the progression of portions of your sermons as a fiction writer would, as scenes. In some, you might do some teaching in the framework of a setting, dialogue, or image. Other sermons might take the shape of an anecdote or first-person experience. But try thinking of your sermon as progressing as a sequence of scenes, each with a specific purpose and sequence. Then make sure your scenes make sense in the order in which you have placed them. Novelist and screenwriter Raymond Obstfeld points out that "the word 'scene' comes from theater, where it describes the action that takes place in a single physical setting." He advises his students to "think of each scene in their work as an inner tube designed to keep the larger work afloat. The more memorable scenes there are, the more we see the entire structure floating in front of us and, therefore, the more we appreciate the whole work. The fewer memorable scenes there are, the quicker that work sinks to the depths of mediocrity."[15]

This would be a good mental exercise for the preacher who fears her sermon may be incoherent. Try stepping from inner tube to inner tube across the river and see if you can navigate the journey without falling into the water.

According to Obstfeld, a scene ought to focus on a specific purpose. Among these purposes are as follows:

- To give the reader information necessary to further the plot
- To show the conflict between characters
- To develop a particular character by highlighting a specific trait or action
- To create suspense[16]

Obstfeld recommends that once we've written a scene, we reread it and ask ourselves four "Focus" questions.

1. The Plot Focus
   The purpose of this scene is to _____.
2. The Character Focus
   When the reader finishes this scene, he should feel

   _____.

3. The Theme Focus
   When the reader finishes this scene, he should think

   _____.

4. The Suspense Focus
   When the reader finishes this scene he should wonder

_____.[17]

When you finish reading a scene, says Obstfeld, ask yourself,

- Is this scene necessary?
- Does it really matter?
- Does whatever happens deserve its own scene?
- Could the information be placed in one of the neighboring scenes?

Skip Press, author of *The Complete Idiot's Guide to Screenwriting*, adds two additional questions for us to ponder with regard to scene and coherence:

- How does the end of this scene propel us into the next one?
- Is this scene memorable apart from the overall movie?[18]

Karl Iglesias, in *Writing for Emotional Impact*, challenges screenwriters to "think of your script as a house of cards, each scene a card. If you can remove a scene, and the house still stands, in other words, if the story still works without it, that scene doesn't belong in your script."[19]

Screenwriter Terry Rossio warns that scenes that aren't needed "die on the screen."[20]

The Sermon That Is Coherent but Boring

Robert C. Dykstra, who teaches pastoral theology at Princeton Theological Seminary, in his book *Discovering a Sermon: Personal Pastoral Preaching*, suggests that the tendency to bore others is a sign of psychological distress. By contrast, the tendency to be bored can be the beginning of a healthy curiosity that leads the preacher into a way of living that Dykstra calls "playing witness to life . . . bearing witness to God's grace at work in life around us."[21]

I started preaching the summer before I started my studies at Duke Divinity School and took a preaching course. I was serving the Page-Roseland Charge, which consisted of two small churches near Aberdeen, North Carolina. All I knew to do was explain things to people and watch their faces. When they looked bored, I'd toss them a story. My sermon form was to lead the congregation on a forced march through a barren wilderness of concepts with periodic stops to distribute candy bars.

That's one way to be boring. There are lots of other ways. I'll leave you to speculate about how I know this. One other way is to suffer from term-paperese, a condition in which we confuse the genre of term paper with that of sermon. Its sermonic symptoms are passive voice, weak adjectives and adverbs, brittle qualifying phrases, obese sentences, and anemic, abstract language. The overall effect is listener numbness.[22]

Another way to be boring is to slip into a humorless, judgmental spiritual state through overwork and underprayer, through a life lacking in imagination and joy. Yet another way is to suffer from anhedonia, a loss of pleasure in living, often cited as a sign of depression. All of these conditions require treatment.

I actually think it's possible to be bored and boring at the same time. If that's our self-diagnosis, fiction writers would counsel us to get a voice or to discover the one we have.

Find Your Voice

We have talked a lot about attentiveness. Different people are attentive to different things. That's why, when I assign twelve students to preach on the same text, I hear twelve different sermons. I hear twelve different voices, because one's voice is a product of that to which one is attentive.

Over the past couple of decades, voice has become a metaphor for one's unique contribution, across a wide number of fields—literature, theology, and preaching among them. In the world of fiction, dust jackets of contemporary novels often mention the word "voice." Publishers regularly put out anthologies featuring voices from distinct groups: southern voices, urban voices, Latin American voices, "under thirty" voices. Awards are given for the best "new voices." Rejection letters sometimes contain the comment, "Sorry, the voice didn't grab us."[23]

What about the preacher's voice? Voice is the unique contribution one makes to the world by bringing one's background and identity to bear on daily experience and expressing it through an artistic medium. Voice does a nice job as a metaphor for uniqueness. It starts with the literal sound made in the vocal cords and becomes a more general metaphor for one's unique expression.

Voice is a combination of what you say and how you sound saying it. It's a product of your slant, your sound, your take, your purpose, your axe to grind, your passion, and your purpose.

Novelist and short-story author Steven Schwartz locates voice in the intersection of the writer's unique experience with that of the larger culture. "The friction here from the self pushing against cultural forces produces a spark from which sound is born: often raw and untutored and shrill to begin with but eventually recognizable to the artistic ear that has been waiting to hear and will create meaning from potent noise." "Voice," says Schwartz, "means knowing why you wrote the story."[24] It's worth repeating, too, that voice is a product of that to which we are attentive.

Novelist Chuck Wachtel, in an essay on narrative voice in fiction, describes the experience of viewing a portrait by Rembrandt as a way of expressing how a reader experiences the author's voice in reading a novel. When viewing a Rembrandt portrait, says Wachtel, your overall impression is of a subject that is clear and in proportion. Then you see the few, small areas that stand out because a beautiful and unnaturally bright light is falling on them. It may be a cuff, the side of a forehead, or a fold of cloth. You don't have to step closer, because you are seeing these small areas as if they were magnified. Wachtel observes that Rembrandt "chose these areas for a reason. There was something of essential importance in them—something more significant, more human, more indicative of what *he* saw, than there was in the other elements of the composition." Wachtel concludes, "Over a century later Van Gogh wrote to his brother Theo that Rembrandt, in his paintings, 'exaggerated the essential and left the obvious vague.' One look at his paintings and we understand exactly what Van Gogh meant."[25]

Your voice as a preacher comes from that to which you are attentive—what you consider, in the interaction between inscape, landscape, and textscape, to be essential.

If we are bored, if we fear that our sermons are boring, maybe we should try lifting our eyes from our trudging feet and tuning in with all five senses to what interests us in life.

The essence of boredom is noninvolvement. If my sermon is boring, it may be because I am not offering listeners opportunities to participate in it: I am telling them about truth, emotions, character transformations, and ideas, rather than inviting them into a plot that involves them in conflict and change, that engages all five of their senses, and that gives them something to figure out along the way.

Find Your Plot

Creative-writing teacher Janet Burroway tells us that many writers want "to express their sensitive observations of life. . . . But your readers want to wonder what happened next. You must master plot, because no matter how profound or illuminating your vision of the world may be, you cannot convey it to those who do not read you."[26] "When editors take the trouble to write a rejection letter to a young author the gist of the letter is 'This piece is sensitive . . . but it is not a *story*.'"[27]

This begs the question, how do we know when we have written a story?

Fiction writers advise us that a story must have three components: conflict, crisis, and resolution. Conflict is the fundamental element of fiction. The consensus of a number of writers is that "only trouble is interesting."[28]

Since a sermon is not a novel, having a plot doesn't mean beginning each sermon with a protagonist who begins a quest, encounters obstacles, and then experiences a resolution, either happy, tragic, or bittersweet. But creative writers would affirm the insight of much contemporary homiletical theory, that there is a deep narrative plotline to sermons that involves conflict and resolution.[29]

Many of the options for imaginative sermon forms that we'll find in chapter 5 fit this flow. The sermons that appear in chapter 6 are from my preaching ministry over the past ten years. In preparing each of them, I don't remember purposely plotting conflict and resolution. Still that plotline runs beneath their surface. For example, "Filled with Fear" begins with an opening scene in which a man is afraid of life; it segues to a teaching portion about the fear of the Lord (=faith in God), and it then resolves into several scenes in which people face life with faith in God.

While sermons don't always unfold like chronological stories with events that move a protagonist from conflict and complication to resolution, they are still often fueled by an underlying dynamic that moves the listener along that path.[30] Fiction writers acknowledge that their forms don't always take the shape of chronological events in order. Something else besides chronology may shape their novel—an arrangement of images, motifs, or even (less frequently) abstractions.[31]

Novelist Madison Smartt Bell describes two basic forms for novels: one is "linear design" and is governed by a chronological sequence of events that fall in order like dominoes. A second he calls "modular design," in which the work is arranged around images, ideas, or events, whose meaning doesn't depend on their chronological sequence.[32]

This reminds me of David Schlafer's 1992 book *Surviving the Sermon*, in which he specifies three means by which a sermon can be unified and by which its contents can be carried through the stages of its plot (the forward-moving dynamic of the sermon): image, story, and argument.[33]

If your sermon is not engaging for listeners or for you, ask yourself, "Do I have, somewhere in it—running through it, underlying it, driving it—three C's: conflict, crisis, and resolution?"

While we're on the subject of not being boring, remember that the best plots include an element of suspense. E. M. Forster in his *Aspects of the Novel* reminds us that Scheherazade, legendary Persian queen and storyteller of *One Thousand and One Nights*, avoided the daily threat of beheading because she knew how to wield the weapon of suspense. She managed to keep the king wondering what would happen next.[34]

Show Me (Don't Just Tell Me)

Show me truth. "Show, don't just tell," is common advice in creative-writing manuals. For preachers it means that we need to provide examples of the truths we are commending, not just expect people to take our word for it. If you are afraid that your sermons may be boring, check to see if they are chock-full of abstract statements with no examples.

Does your sermon consist of a series of statements about God and the life of faith, each followed by conceptual explanation? "We reach a place in life where we realize that we are living a superficial existence." "In our relationship with Christ, God gives us the gift of discovering our deepest identity." "We need to live in such a way that the values of our faith take priority over the values of the world." "The incarnation is God's action to meet us in our grief." "Despite the instances of violence and hatred in the world over the past several months, God is at work in the world bringing redemption and reconciliation." All these statements are edifying and, I believe, true. But we need to give the listener examples, not just expect them to take our word for it.

Try what I call the "generalization buster" exercise. Read through your manuscript and highlight every general statement. In the margin next to it, write, "So what? Where? When? How? Show me."

"We need to live by the values of our faith and not our culture." Show me where and when and in what situation(s). Show me what that would that look like in my life.

"The incarnation of Jesus Christ is God's way of meeting humankind in their grief." Where? When? With what result? What kind of grief? What kind of meeting? Show me.

Show me your character's emotions. Novelists have lots of advice about portraying characters. It is relevant wherever people appear in our sermons, whether we are using a brief contemporary illustration, bringing a biblical character to life, or recounting a personal experience.

John Gardner offers us this advice on use of detail in characterization. "The writer with an accurate eye (and ear, nose, sense of touch, etc.) has an advantage over the writer who does not in that he can tell his story in concrete terms, not just feeble abstractions." He recommends that, instead of telling us that "She felt terrible," we show, by the gesture or look, the nuance of her feelings. An abstract adjective is not much help. He points out that "one can feel sad or happy or bored or cross in 1,000 ways." The precise gesture, on the other hand, pinpoints the feeling. "Good writers may tell about almost anything in fiction except the characters' feelings."[35]

Josip Novakovich commends this approach because it allows the reader (or listener) to participate. His advice to writers is, "In description, directly show what can be seen and allow readers to infer the rest. You must show emotion. Don't just say outright how your characters feel. Give the reader evidence. How do we know that Joan is bored, that Peter is ashamed, that Thomas is skeptical? Show how they look and behave, what their hands are doing, and the reader will infer the emotion."[36] Screenwriter Karl Iglesias suggests that aspiring screenwriters watch silent films to learn how to show instead of tell.[37]

Descriptions keep the writer, as well as the reader, close to the scene. They help her visualize, concretize, and participate in the story.[38]

Maybe you're trying to convey the personality of someone who appears in an illustrative story. Consider this characterization: "He had good qualities. He was committed to his vocation, and he had a hearty love of life. But he had a fault. He became angry easily. He would feel angry whenever someone showed him disrespect. He felt that just because he was a preacher didn't mean he had to take any insult someone wanted to give him. And so he felt angry as he looked at the man standing across from him and contemplated whether or not to hit him."

A fiction writer would recommend a different type of approach, in which the preacher shows how her uncle felt through his actions: "He ran his left hand over the knuckles of his right hand, one by one. One for each insult received. He opened his palm and looked down at his big hand, which could baptize, back slap, and smooth a brow. He closed it into a fist again and halfway raised it toward his adversary."

Show me your character's personality. Use sensory details to describe characters in your sermon. Use details about a person's dress, personal tastes, and mannerisms to indicate their personality. Don't overdo the details. Three are usually enough. The trick is that you are choosing details that suggest more than their literal meaning, details that tie outer manifestations to their inner characters. You are linking details of appearance, dress, personal taste, and mannerisms to the person underneath, allowing us to infer their character and motivations.[39]

Lavonne Mueller and Jerry Reynolds suggest this exercise to practice showing characters' traits rather than just telling about them.

> Look at the following statements. Offer a couple of details regarding the person's appearance and mannerisms that show what the person is like.
>   Carlos has trouble making up his mind.
>   Anita is stingy.
>   Brian is carefree.[40]

Maybe you're describing a biblical character. "He wore the softest robe in the crowd, though no hands reached out to touch it. Head down, he looked even shorter, scurrying toward the tree." We could say much more, but that's probably enough. The reader or listener can figure out that Zacchaeus is the richest person in the crowd, that no one liked him, and that he knew no one liked him. It's the difference between the author putting a label on someone and the character revealing his emotions and personality.

Show me setting. Use sensory details to describe setting in sermons. The vivid description that is the key to showing characters' emotions and personalities is also the key to portraying scenes and settings. The same principles apply. Show listeners details that suggest more than their literal meaning, details that tie the scene or setting to the inner dynamics of the characters in them. Whether you are portraying a biblical setting or a contemporary one, use details that engage all five senses—describe weather, geography, food, smells, textures, place, windows, light, furniture, you name it—to convey concepts and emotional dynamics.

> The smell of martyrs' blood mingled with the dirt of the coliseum floor. The sounds of flames licking at the buildings as Rome burned. A wild glint in an emperor's eyes. The taste of bread and wine as they share their holy meal, but their hands tremble as they reach out to receive it. This is the Gospel of Mark. Probably written at the outset of a persecution, possibly by Nero. It's written in a crucible: this accounts for its high blood pressure, urgent feel, for its stress on

sacrifice, for its terse language. There isn't much time; there is lots of danger. Persecutions are imminent. Are you in or are you out?

When conveying a particular scene, the same rules apply.

> He sat across from me, his face chalky except for the maroon gash over one eye. About to tell me a story I'd heard before and would hear again. Drinks at the bar. Driving his buddy home. Single car accident. Friend in ICU fighting to live. His cut hadn't even needed stitches. He picked up the Bible we kept on the coffee table, his hands brushing off the dust. Somebody had given it to us for our wedding. It was white Naugahyde, with the face of Jesus on it in velveteen. Auburn hair. Limpid blue eyes. He began tracing the face of Jesus, around the chin, the outline of nose, eyes, brow, hair and back again, tracing the face of Jesus.

Says Janet Burroway in *Imaginative Writing*, "If you write in words that evoke the senses, if your language is full of things that can be seen, heard, smelled, tasted, and touched, you create a world your reader can enter." It is the difference between "Not everything that appears to be valuable is actually valuable," and "All that glistens is not gold."[41]

Creative-writing teacher Natalie Goldberg talks about the school essay she had to write in the fall of fifth grade, "What I Did Last Summer." She wrote, "My summer was fun." If she had it to do over again, she says, she would get more specific and concrete with her details. She says she would remember the fiction writer's dictum that "you tell the truth and you depict it in detail." If she had done that, her essay would have read, "My mother dyed her hair red and polished her toenails silver. I was mad for Parcheesi and running in the sprinkler, catching beetles in a mason jar and feeding them grass. My father sat at the kitchen table a lot staring straight ahead, never talking, a Budweiser in his hand."[42]

Goldberg recommends that writers, in their descriptions of places, people, and events, use concrete, significant details: "*Concrete* means that there is an image, something that can be seen, heard, smelled, tasted or touched. *Detail* means that there is a degree of focus and specificity. *Significant* means that the specific image also suggests an abstraction, generalization or judgment."[43]

The relevance of this advice for our sermons is that we need to *focus listener's attention on something in particular* for a *reason* (that pertains to our theme and purpose) by means of an *appeal to one of the senses*. This is how we convey information through vivid detail. We direct our listeners' intellects and emotions toward the meaning of the details.

That is why fiction writers warn us that, while description is important, overdescription is deadly. It diffuses rather than directs the reader's intellect and emotions.

Edith Wharton in *The Writing of Fiction* points out that the traditions of the Theatre Francais used to require that the number of objects on the stage—chairs, tables, even a glass of water on a table—should be limited to the actual requirements of the drama: the chairs must all be sat in, the table carry some object necessary to the action, the glass of water or decanter of wine be a part of the drama.[44] That's a good point to remember when we're tempted to weary our listeners with too much detail. Showing too much is as bad as not showing at all.

Show me concepts by using active verbs and images. Fiction writers warn us that flat writing is full of abstractions. Replace them with nouns that call up sense images and verbs that represent actions we can visualize. The writing comes alive, and at the same time, the ideas and judgments are also present in the images.[45]

> Don't habitually conceal your abilities and talents from those around you.
> "Don't hide your light under a bushel basket."
> A large, impressive visual object cannot generally be concealed from passersby.
> "A city set on a hill cannot be hid."
> Lots of people today are futilely seeking wisdom from illegitimate sources.
> "Are grapes gathered from thorns, or figs from thistles?"

While conceptual thinking is crucial to human communication, sense impressions are what make writing come alive and connect with people's emotions. The physiological reason for this effect is that information taken in through the five senses is processed in the limbic system of the brain, which generates physical responses in the body: heart rate, blood/oxygen flow, muscle reaction, and so forth. Physiological reactions trigger emotional responses. To have an effect on your reader's emotions, you must literally get into the limbic system. You can only do that through the senses.[46]

Whenever you can, convey concepts through images that spark listeners' memories and experiences and which involve all their senses. If you're preaching on the healing of blind Bartimaeus in Mark 10:46–52, convey the concept of "our craving for security" using the metaphor of Bartimaeus's cloak. Convey the concept of "our response to Jesus' call" using Bartimaeus's action of casting it off (not folding it over his arm) and moving toward Jesus.

Use active verbs that can themselves be images. "When he was called by Jesus' messengers, he relinquished the symbol of his former life and moved into the future." How about, "When he heard them call his name, he leapt to his feet, threw off his cloak, coins jingling on the ground, and put one foot in front of the other all the way to Jesus." When we use active verbs rather than passive verbs, listeners can see the actions in their mind's eye, not just be told about them conceptually. Avoid passive verbs in favor of active verbs that "jump-start the mind."[47]

Writers often use ordinary acts and objects to connect with a larger, more universal meaning. A stopped clock can be a metaphor for the death of a character, a bird with broken wings can symbolize the failed hopes of the protagonist. A train that, once in motion, cannot stop, can symbolize events in someone's life. When Shakespeare has the sleepwalking Lady Macbeth try to wash the imagined blood from her hands, this everyday act takes on a larger meaning.[48]

Consider shaping your sermon or portions of your sermon along the contours of metaphor. There is always a concept inherent in a metaphor. Biblical texts teem with metaphors we don't have to manufacture. "They are like trees planted by streams of water, which yield their fruit in its season, and their leaves do not wither" (Ps. 1:3); "Now you are the body of Christ and individually members of it" (1 Cor. 12:27); "See, I am setting a plumb line in the midst of my people Israel" (Amos 7:8); "How great a forest is set ablaze by a small fire! And the tongue is a fire" (James 3:5). The biblical fields are so ripe for the metaphor harvest that it's hard to stop finding examples once you start.

Some metaphors are not so obvious, but lie within or beneath the surface of a text in context. Lying in a ditch watching feet go by, helpless to save ourselves. There is a metaphor for the human condition you might discern in the Good Samaritan. The twelfth chapter of Hebrews introduces the metaphor of a race. A preacher could offer a personal experience of participating in a race or walk, offering observations on the varying levels of fitness of the participants, place in the pack, purpose of the event, crucial role of those handing out water and calling encouragement, and so forth, as a way of teaching insights into our journey of faith together.

Think what concepts you could convey by means of connecting the following actions or objects with deeper meanings: "Under his wings you will find refuge" (Ps. 91:4); the tree Zacchaeus climbed (Luke 19); a "straight path in which they shall not stumble" (Jer. 31:9); a woman gathering manna off the ground, holding the flakes in the palm of her hand (Exod. 16). The fields of biblical texts and your own experience are ripe for the metaphorical harvest.

The Sermon That Is Interesting but Offers False Teaching

I'm including this fourth section, not because I think you are in danger of preaching sermons that offer false teachings, but to give you some ammunition against their seductive appeal. What is the impact of a steady diet of "false teaching" sermons on a congregation? Mood swings; between false optimism and false guilt.

Over the years I have heard sermons featuring eight patterns of false teachings. I have probably also unintentionally preached a few, may God forgive me. I judge them to be false because, in my view, they are not in keeping with the teachings of the full witness of the Bible (as opposed to individual prooftexts). Nor do they do justice to the complexity of life as we live it. The eight patterns of false teachings are as follows:

- If you had more faith, you would be healed and your problems would disappear.
- Faith automatically brings happy endings, healings, job opportunities, and satisfying relationships.
- Living faithfully is a very simple matter.
- God has everything all worked out if we would just cooperate.
- Misfortunes come directly from God as punishments or teaching moments.
- There are no accidents.
- All suffering is a cross we must bear to be faithful disciples.
- Faith is a personal matter. Talking about issues of public life in the pulpit is mixing faith and politics.

A fiction writer would critique these false teachings on the basis of their inadequate plots. The effect of each of these false teachings is to eliminate the complexity and tension from the plot of the life of faith. The so-called prosperity gospel, which is by no means unique to the late twentieth and early twenty-first centuries, teaches that if you think the right kind of thoughts and pray the right kind of prayers, God will pour rich blessings upon you, most of them material. New Age philosophies that promise that the universe yearns to give you your heart's desire are in a similar vein.[49]

Making an Entrance, Staying on Track, and Knowing When to Leave: What's the Story?

As we've pointed out, novels can have many different sequences. There is a lively diversity of opinion on plot among fiction writers. Our discussion here is limited to a very brief description of the basic three-act structure that is centuries old. Sometimes referred to as the "character arc," it's not the only story structure, and it has many variations. You'll recognize it, I'm sure.

Nineteenth-century German critic Gustav Freitag analyzed plot in terms of a pyramid of five actions: an exposition (which sets the stage, introducing characters, situation, and setting), followed by a complication (or *nouement*, a "knotting up" of the situation characterized by rising action or tension), leading to a crisis, which is followed by a "falling action" or anticlimax, resulting in a resolution (or denouement, "unknotting").[50]

This translates into the three-part dramatic structure. In act 1 you introduce your setting, characters, and situation (conflict) that drives the main character from their "normal" life toward some conflicting situation. This is called by various names, including inciting incident, catalyst, trigger, or the disturbance.[51]

In act 2, the character encounters various obstacles and antagonists as the conflict develops.

Near the end of act 2 or the beginning of act 3, there is the climax, in which the hero draws on the wisdom he has learned and takes a decisive action that brings the story to a conclusion. Act 3 is the resolution of loose threads and a view of the outcome.

What follows is some basic advice from fiction writers on beginnings, middles, and endings of sermons.

Making an Entrance

First, realize that the creative process is such that you may write your sermon's opening last. A story or image that you have placed later in the sermon may jump to the head of the line. Be open to that happening. The ancient Greek teachers of public speaking recommended that the opening of a speech needed to arouse interest. As a preaching professor I often advise students to make a promise (overt or strongly implied) at the beginning of the sermon, a promise of what listeners will get if they stick with your sermon to the end. Not just any promise will do. It has to be something people want enough to keep listening. Fiction writers would challenge us in the opening of our sermon to introduce a theme, a story, a person, or a situation in which listeners can see themselves, whether they want to or not.

Here is an example that doesn't work because it makes a promise that only history buffs will care if you keep:

> Scholars have struggled with identifying Paul's thorn in the flesh (2 Corinthians 12:1–10). This morning we are going to examine the options and decide on the most likely one given the literary and historical evidence.

This opening makes a promise more relevant to most listeners:

> A person in anguish over a chronic, excruciating problem at the core of his life. That was Paul in the first century for a reason he does not reveal to us. This is many of us this morning for reasons we may not have revealed to anyone else. What was the thorn in his flesh that drove him into the arms of a strong and loving God? We may not find the answer to that question, but along the way we may find something even more important.

Fiction writer Nancy Kress says that every story makes a promise to the reader—actually, two promises, one emotional and one intellectual, because the function of stories is to make us feel and think. "The emotional promise is this: Read this and you'll be entertained, or thrilled, or scared, or titillated, or saddened, or nostalgic, or uplifted, but always absorbed." The intellectual promise can take one of three forms or some combination of them:

1. See this world from a different perspective.
2. Have your current beliefs about the world confirmed.
3. Learn of a different, more interesting world.[52]

Fiction writers tell us that we need to establish empathy between your readers and your main character at the outset. Screenwriter Robert

McKee distinguishes between sympathetic and empathetic. Sympathetic means likeable. Empathetic means "like me."[53] Empathy is different from sympathy. Sympathy says, "I like the main character." Empathy says, "I'm like the main character," and not necessarily in a way I want to admit. It could be a similarity in problem faced, unsavory secret, personality trait, and so on. In any case, establish empathy at the outset. Present a character or situation in which the listeners can see themselves whether they want to or not.

Raymond Obstfeld gives these two contrasting examples for an opening of a story:

"Bill walked into the diner, sat at the counter and scanned the menu for something not too greasy."

"'Someone's sitting there,' the man in the uniform said as Bill started to straddle the stool."

Obstfeld has students in his novel-writing class try to write an opening sentence that guarantees the reader will want to read the rest of the paragraph. The secret of a good opening is that it must compel the writer as much as the reader. To do this you should think of opening lines as a separate entity from the scene (sermon) itself.[54]

The feature of the opening of a story or novel that "hooks" the reader's interest so he or she will want to keep reading is often called the "narrative hook."

The most common and hackneyed opening line for the short stories of novice writers is "The alarm clock rang." Apparently, if a writer doesn't know where her story begins, she simply starts at the beginning of the day of the story.[55]

The problem with that opening is it has no narrative hook. Narrative hooks can take many forms. A sermon or novel could start in the middle of a dramatic scene so listeners have to figure out what's going on. The term *in medias res* (in the middle of things) refers to the technique of starting a story in the middle of a dramatic event and filling in the backstory with flashbacks. If I were preaching on Philippians 2:1–11, I could start in the middle like this:

> They grab his arms, straining them at the sockets, pulling him to his feet. Was that sword at the soldier's side meant for his neck? Now their hands are unlocking his shackles, shoving him out the door— he stumbles on his unused legs. It's too bright out here after all these months. No food. No coin. But who cares? Freedom!

Short-story writers use this technique effectively to draw the reader in by making them curious as to what went before and what will come after. Alice Munro begins her story "Miles City, Montana" with the line, "My father came across the field carrying the body of the boy who had been drowned." Robert Olen Butler begins his story "A Good Scent from a Strange Mountain," with this line: "Ho Chi Minh came to me again last night, his hands covered with confectioners' sugar."[56]

Other narrative hooks could be mysterious settings, an intriguing character, or an enigmatic statement. You be the judge of what would hook your listeners.

Remember that there are a number of ways to begin a sermon besides the deductive method of stating the theme of the sermon right at the outset. Fiction writers, as well as much contemporary advice about preaching, warn us that the downside of that opening gamut is that it is predictable and boring.

If you begin with the biblical world, you need to quickly let listeners know, even if only by a phrase or sentence, that it connects with their lives, as I do in the "thorn in the flesh" example above. "This is many of us this morning. . . ."

If we begin with some issue or story from our contemporary world, we need to show a connection to the text or an aspect of the text. Suppose I started the "thorn" sermon with an anecdote about a chronically ill person. I could frame his condition as a "thorn in the flesh" as a connector with Paul's experience.

Josip Novakovich suggests several options for openings in his book *Fiction Writer's Workshop*. In what follows I illustrate his options using Philippians 2:1–11, where Paul is in prison, possibly at Caesarea, writing to the Philippians and recalling the words of a doxology to Christ (called the Christ Hymn [vv. 6–11]).

We can begin with setting. If I begin my sermon with a scene of Paul in prison, I remember I need to use the setting to appeal to the senses and to set out the theme of the sermon.

> Paul in a dim cell. With thoughts shadowed by pain, loneliness, dread of imminent death. Cold. Stench from not washing. No little travel-sized toiletries provided by the hotel on a fluted tray by a sink. No sink. No sound but his own raspy breathing and the moans of fellow prisoners in adjacent cells. No song. But wait, one comes into his head— what is it? It sounded familiar to him . . . what were the words?

We can begin with an idea. Novakovich warns that this runs the risk of being dry.

> It's the rare person who, in a situation of extreme personal suffering, can focus on someone else's pain.

We can begin with a strong sensation.

> Bands of raw skin around his ankles. Crusted blood. How many more days must he wear these shackles?

Begin with a need or motive.

> As the door to his cell rattled, Paul forced himself to think: "This is it—they're letting me go." He couldn't afford to think the opposite. Not now.

Begin with a symbolic object.

> One ray of light. Through the barred, high window. Just one. That was all he needed.

Begin with a character portrait.

> He sat leaning against the corner of the cell. Hair lank and matted, robe grimy, arms folded, head up, eyes gleaming with hope. . . .

Begin with a question.

> How can he think about them at a time like this?

Begin with the character's thoughts.

> *I can hear a melody going through my head. Now what are those words?* thought Paul.

Begin with a prediction.

> He could never have known, as he sat in that cell, how far into future times and places the letter he was writing would make its way.

Begin with an anecdote (from then or now). The preacher could start with an anecdote that relates to the theme she has discerned in the text.[57]

Staying on Track

"Throughline" is a term borrowed from films. It means the main plotline of your story, the one that answers the question, "What happens to the protagonist?" In sermons, it's our theme, what the sermon is about in one sentence. Suppose I'm preaching on Matthew 8:18–27, Jesus stilling the storm at sea. Suppose my focus or theme sentence is this: "Our faith grows when, in the high gales of life, we turn to *Jesus* and find that he is present and able to help us."

After my opening and before my ending comes the middle. That's where I used to lead the congregation on the forced march through a series of concepts and, when they looked bored, I'd toss them a story to alleviate the tedium.

There are myriad ways to shape the middle of a sermon, too numerous to go into here. The classic three-part story form would tell us to arrange scenes with heightening excitement leading up to a climax and then a resolution. We don't always have to do that. The next chapter offers you lots of options for what to do in the middle. But try thinking of the middle of your sermon as something other than a conceptual wasteland. As a listener I deserve to be simultaneously intrigued and informed. So teach me concepts in scenes.

Scene It: Teach through Scenes

Whenever you teach listeners a concept, put it in a scene or setting and show it to them. They will learn something, but it will be in a framework they can remember. Suppose I want to teach a theological concept in a sermon—that the human Jesus and the divine Jesus were one.

I might tell the story of my childhood church in which the back window was a huge, floor-to-ceiling, double–paned, stained-glass window. On the left pane was the well-known Jesus kneeling in anguish in Gethsemane with the red tear that shimmered on sunny days. On the right was Jesus resurrected and ascending, serene and confident. So, naturally, a five-year-old girl spends most of the service standing on the pew looking at the back wall, head bobbing from pane to pane, man to man, wondering, *Why doesn't that happy man help that sad man?*

Use the imagination that you've cultivated in scanning your inscape, textscape, and landscape to "scene" your concepts. It won't dumb them down. It will clarify them and make them more memorable.

There is a game called "Scene It" that calls on players to identify scenes from recent movies. Creative writers would encourage us to create new scenes in our sermons. I stated in the introduction my conviction that now, more than ever, people need sermons that teach them something. The scene is an ideal vehicle for teaching that holds listeners' interest. Scenes involve characters, setting, dialogue, and often, conflict. A scene has the potential to convey information and touch emotions.

Suppose you want to convey that each of the four Gospel writers has a different focus on what it means to be a disciple. Have them sitting in a booth at the Allen Café (I live in Allen, Texas. You can substitute your town) and offer a dialogue in which each expresses that focus for themselves. Throw in a detail about what each one orders off the menu (that expresses their inner personality) and a pinch of conflict over whose focus is the best, and you've got a teaching scene.

Do you want to teach listeners about the postexilic setting in which the book of Proverbs was collated? You can give a history lesson straight up, but it will be more effective to scene it.

> Smoke from the burned temple wafts upward. The palace is empty and the yard scruffy. The king is long gone—deported by the Babylonians. No temple, no king. Who are we?
>
> Here is a guy sitting alone at a dining room table piled with food engaged in an eating contest in which he is the only contestant. Here is woman sitting alone with an empty bottle working on a second. Here are two married people checking into a motel together—married, but not to each other. Here is a man approaching another man in a bar with a pool cue, his face red and heated. People embroiled in anger, adultery, substance abuse—that's what happens when a community struggles with the loss of identity and dignity as the Israelites after the exile struggled with the loss of king and temple.
>
> Where to turn to regain identity and dignity? How about the book of Proverbs, with its no-nonsense notion of the two paths: the path of folly (that leads to death) and the path of wisdom (that leads to life)? The book of Proverbs—with its series of sayings that commend trust in God; self-control with regard to physical appetites, tongue, and temper; and respect for the poor—is tailor-made to restore order to a culture in a time of chaos.

I want to keep playing "Scene it" as I explore the teaching power of scenes in my future sermons.

Imagine That! Teach through Images

Use images to teach concepts. Nudity is inappropriate in the pulpit. So don't leave your concepts standing naked before the congregation. Clothe a concept with an image. Whenever you are trying to teach a concept, ask yourself, *How can I use an image to express this idea?* Jesus is present and able to help me. The image is right there for us in the text. Jesus is in your boat, ready to still your storm (Matt. 8:26).

Suppose I'm trying to talk about how we don't always want to respond in the same way to situations. Well, put an avocado and a banana on a plate. You don't respond to both the same way. You don't consume the interior of each fruit and throw away the exterior.

Now we're thinking like the sages of Proverbs, searching the realms of nature and human relationships for patterns of divine presence and action. Don't interfere in somebody else's business. "Like somebody who takes a passing dog by the ears is one who meddles in the quarrel of another" (Prov. 26:17).

Articulate the concept within the image. Whenever there is an image in a text, ask yourself, what concept informs it? What concept informs the picture of a tree planted by streams of water that will not be moved? Or the valley of dry bones that are rattling to their bony feet and taking on flesh and health? Resolve to keep the two together, images or metaphors and concepts. That would make for more interesting preaching; preaching that informs teaches delightfully and delights informatively.

Making an Exit: When and How

F. A. Rockwell, in his article titled "How Not to Fizzle a Finale," recommends, as do a number of authors, planning the ending first. Use your first fresh inspiration to plan your ending first.[58]

Novelist Katherine Anne Porter wrote, "If I didn't know the ending of a story, I wouldn't begin. I always write my last lines, my last paragraph, my last page first, and then I go back and work towards it. I know where I'm going. I know what my goal is."[59]

Every story (sermon) has several possible endings. Here is a checklist for determining an effective ending for a story (sermon).

1. It satisfies. It does not cheat or frustrate the listener/reader. It answers or at least addresses the questions raised in the sermon.
2. It fits the mood and subject matter and inspires a specific emotional reaction from your listener/reader.
3. It packs a surprise of some kind. It must contain a twist the listener/reader couldn't foresee.
4. It is logical. Even if the solution or ending is a complete surprise, it must be credible and convincing because you have planted subtle signposts along the way.[60]

Rockwell offers this specific advice about endings: "Whatever your ending, it shouldn't be skimpy, leaving too much for the reader to figure out; and it shouldn't be overloaded with pedantically presented information and description. Nor should it ramble on after solving a major problem, or focus on minor characters." He further advises that we not leave the characters' relationships the same as in the beginning, or give away the solution before it happens.[61] I would add that we ought not promise a tidy solution to an issue that is still not completely resolved at this point.

Rockwell offers a couple of different types of endings for short stories that the preacher can apply to sermons:

> One is the summation ending. I call it the "that's all she wrote ending." This ending is a solution ending, a problem solved (the brave reporter exposes corruption in city hall), a desired outcome attained (the hero gets the girl). To turn to the sad side, perhaps the lovers are reunited as one of them lies on her death bed (most operas), or a final scene in which all the characters are sprawled (dead) on the stage as the curtain goes down (Shakespearean tragedy).[62]

Another is the "go figure" ending. This type of ending, says Rockwell, "annoys the unimaginative reader who wants the writer to do all the work."[63] In this kind of ending the author has, in the story (or sermon), posed a problem and developed it, but leaves the solution up to the reader. You could, for example, end a sermon on the Prodigal Son parable this way:

> We are left at the end of the parable, not sure whether the older brother will go into the banquet hall or not. Maybe the affront to his sense of fairness will overpower his yearning for the forgiveness and joy that lie within the banquet hall. Maybe he will go off to the barn

and fork some hay to work off his frustrations, the sound of the fes-
tivities accosting his ears. Or maybe his yearning for the love that lies
within the banquet hall will overcome all else, and he will enter into
the joy of a God who rejoices over the return of every lost child.[64]

Yet another possibility is what Rockwell calls the "antennae ending."
This ending leaves a problem unsolved at the end, but sends feelers into
the future, promising hopeful possibilities. Rockwell cites as a famous
antennae ending Scarlett O'Hara's worry-about-Rhett-tomorrow phi-
losophy at the end of *Gone with the Wind*. The ending of the sermon
"Filled with Fear" in chapter 6 is an example of this kind of ending, as is
"Suppertime at the Gospel Café." Everything is not resolved, but hope is
offered for handling future fearful events.

The twist ending offers a surprise. The storyteller or preacher has
placed signposts along the way so the listener or reader, while taken by
surprise, still finds the ending credible. The ending to the sermon illus-
trates a surprise ending.

Choose the ending for your sermon that satisfies, fits the mood and
subject matter, and is appropriate—one that springs a surprise; is logical
according to the people, events, images, and ideas you've presented so
far; and that inspires the reader with a promise. Your ending needs to
tie up all the loose ends and harvest all the dramatic and emotional seeds
you've planted in the beginning and cultivated in the middle. Plant, cultivate, harvest.[65]

Speaking of knowing when to leave, it's time to stop for the day. One
can only take so much good advice at a time. I thank all of our fiction
writing consultants. They drift away in groups of three or four to a local
café to share ideas into the wee hours. At least that's what I imagine them
doing—wearing berets and staying up later than I do.

There is just one more field trip I'd like you to go on with me. I'll be by
for you tomorrow morning at 9 a.m. We're going to the Sermon Chefs
Convention at the fairgrounds. Wear comfortable shoes.

Chapter Five

Sermon Chefs

Recipes from Contemporary Preachers

My new favorite cooking show is *Iron Chef*. It originated in Japan, where it was called "The Ironmen of Cooking" and aired from 1993 to 1999. It was picked up by the Food Network, dubbed in English, and became a cult favorite with viewers. Its host is the flamboyant Takeshi Kaga, known on the show as Chairman Kaga. The story behind the show is that Kaga constructed a cooking arena in his castle called "Kitchen Stadium." There, visiting chefs from around the world compete against his Gourmet Academy, led by his four Iron Chefs, each specializing in a particular kind of cuisine: French, Italian, Chinese, and Japanese.

The introduction to the show features a cavernous room, lit with flickering torches. While Wagnerian music plays in the background, the announcer says dramatically: "Nearly a decade ago, a man's fantasy became a reality in a form never seen before, a giant cooking arena called Kitchen Stadium. The motivation behind spending his fortune to create Kitchen Stadium was to encounter new original cuisines that could be called true artistic creations. To realize his dream he started choosing the top chefs from various styles of cooking whom he called 'the invincible men of culinary skills, the Iron Chefs.'"

Each Iron Chef is then spotlighted at the front, supplying viewers with their culinary credentials, current specialty, and claim to fame. Then, the famed "key ingredient," which has been concealed behind a screen, is revealed with a flourish, and the chefs and their sous-chefs start to work.

Amid gleaming stoves and ranges, food processors, shining pots and pans, glinting knives, and jars of fresh spices, chefs have one hour to improvise a multicourse meal around a theme ingredient that must be present in each dish. The judges then determine which chef was able to

79

"best express the unique qualities of the theme ingredient," using the criteria of taste, presentation, and originality. Some theme ingredients have been cranberries, lamb, cod roe, asparagus, papayas, tofu, river eel, bell peppers, summer corn, peaches, prawns, lobster, and eggs.

So here we are at the fairgrounds at this year's Annual Sermon Chefs Cooking Convention. It's inspired by *Iron Chef*, but it's not a contest. Our role is to go from station to station, gathering ideas and samples and recipe cards.

Literary Cuisine: "The Novel Sermon"

Charles Rice, a pioneer in the use of imagination in twentieth-century preaching, is at his cooking station. On his kitchen counter is his book *Interpretation and Imagination*, with four sermons that illustrate his method. Each of them is shaped by a poem, a novel, a play, or a movie.[1] On the counter Chef Rice also has an array of books of poems, novels, and plays, marked with colorful bookmarks. We walk closer to catch what he is saying: "All serious literature is theologically valuable, and it is only when that is understood that any literature is homiletically available."[2]

Quite a crowd is gathering around his station, drawn by the delicious smells of his literary ingredients. Trained in the kitchen of theologian Paul Tillich, Rice shares his savoring of literature as an expression of our "ultimate concern," whereby we seek to discover the ground and purpose of our lives. Religion and literature, for Rice, as for Tillich, are both expressions of this existential exploration. Rice favors sermon recipes that combine the two key ingredients of literature and Scripture.[3]

It is in the uninhibited encounter with literature that a sermon may be conceived and in theological reflection that it is formed.
—Charles Rice

By preaching sermons based on literary works, we imitate literary artists' imagination-evoking forms of communication—story, indirection, personal involvement, self-revelation, plot, character, and metaphor—in our sermons. We preach in a way that evokes listeners' own experiences rather than prescribing propositions.[4]

It's time to move to the next station, but before we do, we pick up a recipe card. Glancing at it, we wonder at first why it is so general, but then realize that Rice wants us to choose the specific ingredients.

The "Novel" Sermon

If you start your sermon recipe with a text, find a piece of literature that illuminates it, that shares its ultimate concern: its lament at what human life has come to and its vision for what human life could be, lived with God.

If you start your sermon recipe with a literary work, discern its theological import: what seems most important to the characters, what encourages and impedes their attaining it, and what kind of life results from the quest. In shaping your sermon, follow the flow of the literary artistic work, pulling through it a thread of scriptural insight.

As we move to the next station, we reflect on how the recipes Rice first published in 1970 could still be nutritious today. Today, the preacher can't assume that people are reading literature as Rice assumed they were in 1970. But preaching on a well-chosen novel that has relevance for a congregation could help reverse the trend. The plot and characters of the novel become the vehicle for an aspect of the biblical text to be explored—perhaps the will to persevere and take risks in the name of love in *The Brief Wondrous Life of Oscar Wao* by Junot Díaz; or guilt, betrayal, and redemption in *The Kite Runner* by Khaled Hosseini; or the beauty of family loyalty in *Run* by Ann Patchett. Such a sermon needs to supply all the information needed so that the sermon makes sense to someone who has not read the novel.

Inductive Cuisine: "The Image-Based Sermon"

Next we visit Chef Fred Craddock's station. The counter is littered with a bag of flour, a bag of sugar, a box of salt, and a bottle of olive oil. A dog-eared copy of his *As One without Authority* is on the kitchen counter. As we approach, he is stirring a crock full of thick, bubbly, sour-smelling batter. As he stirs, he explains why he favors cooking with images. He begins by explaining that images, the fruit of the imagination, are the catalyst for changes of mind and heart: "Long after a man's [sic] head has consented to a preacher's idea, the old images may still hang in the heart. But not until that image is replaced is he really a changed man. . . . This change takes time because the longest trip a person takes is that from the head to heart."[5]

Craddock adds some flour and water to the bubbly batter. He explains that sourdough bread is made by using a small amount of "starter" dough, sometimes known as "the mother sponge," which contains a yeast culture, and mixing it with new flour and water. He tells us he will save part of this resulting dough to use as the starter for the next batch. As long as the starter dough is fed flour and water daily, the sourdough mixture can stay at room temperature indefinitely and remain healthy and usable.

He tells us to begin our sermon with a concrete idea as our starter dough, waiting until later to add conceptual conclusions to the batter. He notes that for some cooks, images and stories are only garnish to put on top of a main course made out of ideas. But in his bakery, images and stones are an integral part of the recipe. As he vigorously stirs the batter, he reminds us that not just any image will do. Images need to be drawn from the worlds familiar to us and our congregation, "specific and concrete; economical in their use of words, and expressed in the preacher's own language."[6]

He dumps the batter onto a floured board and begins to knead and shape it. He recommends that we shape our sermon in the form of a journey of discovery, in which the listeners identify with the images and events and thoughts of the unfolding sermon and reach their own conclusions, new perspectives, and decisions by the end of the sermon. He turns and kneads the sermon dough some more. He advises us to create a sermon *with* the congregation, gathering ingredients—experiences, images, bits of knowledge—keeping them in suspense until the end as to exactly what kind of bread we're making. Listeners have both the right and the ability to eat part of it there and take the rest home.

Recipe Idea: Romans 5:1–5 *au* Craddock

Preaching a Chef Craddock sermon on Romans 5 could take the title "Forgot Your Password?" It could begin with several images of what happens when we forget our password, our garage door opener, our credit card, or our access code. When we are stressed we tend to forget simple things like passwords.

Then the sermon could move to experiences and images of denied access to everyday goods. From there it could move into experiences of denied access to deeper spiritual realities dealt with in this passage: sharing in the glory of God to the point that we can even boast in our sufferings.

The conclusion: faith in Jesus Christ is the password we have forgotten when we try to access God's glory by our efforts alone. Remembering our faith in Christ's grace opens to us the mysterious journey from suffering to hope. We can boast in our hope of sharing the glory of God. We can even boast in our sufferings.

Contemplative Cuisine: "The Prayer-Shaped Sermon"

As we approach Patricia Wilson-Kastner's kitchen station, we notice two things. There is a well-worn copy of Eugene Lowry's book *The Homiletical Plot* open on the cutting board next to a copy of her own *Imagery for Preaching* (1989). A picture of St. Ignatius of Loyola is hanging beside the sink.

Chef Wilson-Kastner is seated in a comfortable wing chair in the corner of her kitchen station. Next to her chair is a small table with a cross, a well-worn Bible, and a lit candle. We have walked up just in time to hear her begin an explanation of how she prepares for her sermon recipes.

While we are interested in her introductory comments, we wonder when she is going to get up and start cooking. She suggests that our sermons should be shaped like our prayerful interaction with the imagery of the biblical text. Gesturing toward the picture of St. Ignatius on the wall, she recommends a form of biblically rooted prayer based on his sixteenth-century *Spiritual Exercises* as a way of both preparing to preach and shaping the sermon. The preacher enters imaginatively into the world of the text and listens for divine direction. This becomes the shape of the preaching event itself.

She goes on to describe Ignatian prayer, as set forth in *The Spiritual Exercises of St. Ignatius*, as a process that involves the use of the imagination, sensory awareness, intellectual insights and reflection, affective response, and quiet listening for God's word. Wilson-Kastner describes preparing a prayer-shaped sermon as a four-step process. She is still sitting down in her chair, and we are becoming increasingly impatient for her to get up and start cooking. Instead she describes the prayer/sermon preparation process.

1. *First, we pray for grace from God to be fully oriented in witness and worship to God.* We establish our relation to the physical time and place in which the biblical event takes place. Ignatius explicitly encourages us to use our imaginations.

2. *Second, we ask God what will help us pray in this place.* Wilson-Kastner uses the example of the meeting of Mary and Elizabeth in Luke 1:39–45. We might ask God for faith to participate in their excitement, for example. We enter into the event, applying memory, mind, and will. The full exercise of our senses and imagination is essential to bring us as living participants into the biblical scene. We can imagine ourselves as a bystander at the event. We can address the characters. We can ask questions. We give ourselves time to become part of their world, to let the characters take on their own life and share it with us. We may see pictures, hear words, recall quotations, and become aware of the fresh relevance of something that has seemed familiar to us. A particular image may become the center that evokes emotion and thought in us.[7]

3. *Third, we reflect on what we hear and experience.* This process involves imagination, intellect, and will. Ignatius wants us to ask, *How does this encounter move me? What does it show me about myself I'd like to change, to strengthen, to be constant in? What do I want to do as a result?*[8]

4. *Finally, we end our prayer time with specific connections between God's word to us and our life and activities.* Says Wilson-Kastner, "In Ignatius' view, prayer always connects the biblical world, the active Word of God to us through the Scriptures, with our life."[9]

Wilson-Kastner is convinced that the shape and movement of this image-based, sensory prayer (felt need, entry into the world of the text, encounter that brings internal transformation and external impact on our lives) does not end with the time of prayer, but continues directly into the form of the sermon.[10]

Now she finally stands up and moves toward the counter on which there is an open Bible and a copy of Eugene Lowry's *The Homiletical Plot.* Holding up his book she tell us that her understanding of sermon form is drawn from what has come to be called "the Lowry loop." This is a sermon recipe that begins with the identification of a tension or conflict in the text or contemporary world, its resolution by means of an aspect of the text or the Gospel, followed by a demonstration of its impact on the life of the preacher and her community.

Wilson-Kastner's version of Lowry's loop makes an image from the text the feature that integrates the plot. She reminds us that in our imaginative prayer experience, images from texts often grasp us and pull us in, becoming the focal point of our encounter with God through the text. An image can become the means by which the body, mind, and spirit are brought into contact with God's dialogue with us through the text. She says, "Any living encounter with imagery springing from Scripture is revelatory and thus involves a plot. As one perceives the image and allows it to affect one, tension, change and transformation are involved."[11] This is Lowry's loop with an image at the helm.

As we listen, she rolls up her sleeves and turns to Psalm 40. As she holds up the Bible, a huge boulder emerges from the psalm and rests on the kitchen counter. "Hello," she greets it playfully, then turns to us. "Apparently someone wants me to begin this sermon with the Rock. Rather than tell my people that God is reliable and stable, I'm to introduce them to the Rock, from the perspective of their senses, inviting them to engage with how it looks and feels. I am to allow the sermon's theological, existential reflection and ethical guidance to emerge from people's initial encounter with this image."

She looks at us. "That means that listeners would participate in the reality of the stability and reliability and power of the rock, then move to God as Rock, rather than have those ideas imposed on them at the beginning of the sermon."

She smiles at us, as if to say, "Move along, now." Taking her mixing bowl and her Bible, she returns to her prayer chair.

Before we move on, we collect two recipe cards to take home with us so we'll remember how to shape sermons by putting Ignatian prayer in conversation with Eugene Lowry's *Homiletical Plot.*

Recipe Idea: Psalm 40 à la Wilson-Kastner

This is a two-act play in which the first two movements focus on the biblical world, the second two on the contemporary world:
The psalmist's conflict
The stability of God as Rock
Our conflict
The stability of God our Rock today.[12]

Sermon Sample: Dives and Lazarus à la Wilson-Kastner

This recipe using the rich man and Lazarus parable from Luke 17 has four parts: tension then, tension now, resolution then, and resolution now.

The biblical world and our world alternate in a four-part movement:

- Tension or trouble in the text
- Example from life today
- Gospel/textual resolution
- How that looks in life today

The tension in the text is embodied in the image of the unbridgeable gap between rich and poor in Jesus' day.

That gap in life today became clear to Wilson-Kastner when she attended a conference in her hometown of Dallas. She stayed in a luxury hotel but visited the now run-down neighborhood where she grew up.

The Gospel/textual resolution is the possibility that there could have been a different ending to the story. Dives and Lazarus could have helped one another. The Eucharist for Wilson-Kastner serves as an image of encounter and healing. God's grace given to us in Jesus Christ forms a bridge between the rich and the poor.

How that would look today? She offers specific manifestations of healing the division between rich and poor. We are free, as Dives and Lazarus once were, to meet and be healed or to remain alienated.[13]

Contemplative Cuisine: "The Spiral Sermon"

We approach the cooking station of teacher of preaching Eunjoo Mary Kim. She has anthologies of fables, koans, and proverbs spread on the kitchen counter. Alongside them is her own book *Preaching the Presence of God: A Homiletic from an Asian American Perspective* (1999). We step up closer so we can hear what she is saying. As she talks, she is preparing a Korean sushi recipe (*gim-bahp*).

As she deftly rolls the rice that has been steamed with vinegar and sugar (*bahp*) around morsels of meat and vegetables, she recommends that preachers consider preaching as "consensus-oriented conversation" and that we allow room for silence and meditation in our sermons. She suggests an imaginative form for preaching that she baptizes "the Spiral." It is a sermon that circles several times around a central focus and finally, at the end, touches it. As she stretches the seaweed sheet (*gim*) around the rice and filling, she gives us a sense of why this sermon recipe fits the congregations she has in mind.

Just as a mother prepares a meal with love and concern for the family, so the preacher begins the preparation for preaching with love and concern for the congregation. . . . Just as the mother does her meal planning for some period of time . . . so the preacher needs to make a preaching plan. . . . Fresh ingredients make the food savory and nutritious. Likewise, choosing a text and giving it new meaning on the basis of the particular experience of the congregation are essential to preparing for spiritual preaching. Such diverse cooking methods as steaming, boiling, grilling, or frying and the use of various sauces or special spices allow a variety of dishes to emerge. . . . For example, with tomato sauce food becomes Italian; with curry, Indian; with soy sauce and cornstarch, Chinese; and with red pepper and sesame oil, Korean. Likewise, sermons become diverse by adopting diverse sermonic forms and seasoning with various cultural additions and expressions.
—*Eunjoo Mary Kim*[14]

Kim suggests that sermons imitate the indirect mode of communication. In Asian American churches, this approach is especially needed and appreciated, since indirect communication is familiar to people through Buddhist stories and koans, Confucian sayings and anecdotes, and folk plays and fables. All these, like Jesus' parables and sayings, are forms of indirect communication to which the listeners must contribute for meaning making to occur.

The Spiral is different from the three-point deductive sermon primarily aimed at teaching concepts to the intellect. It is different from the sermon that articulates current assumptions, replaces them with a biblical affirmation, and culminates in a finale of emotional celebration. It is different from the inductive sermon that withholds its "aha" moment until the end. In each of the Spiral's circlings, the mind, will, and heart are addressed. In any of them, a moment of insight can occur.[15]

As we move on to the next cooking station, we take one of the recipe cards set out on the counter to take home.

Recipe Idea: Spiral Sermon

As an example of a Spiral sermon, Kim uses a Buddhist funeral sermon. In the first circling, the preacher presents death at the existential level as a human karmic event and with compassionate words paints the picture of humans' collective, inescapable predicament. In the second circling, the preacher depicts death at a personal level, detailing its psychological and emotional impact and ministering to listeners' emotions. In the third circling, death is viewed beyond sorrow in a community context as an experience through which we experience our essential humanity. That is the significance of the Buddhist doctrine of interdependence. In the fourth circling, the preacher tells an anecdote of how Sakayamuni Buddha reached out to a young mother who had lost her child. The last circling is followed by meditation.[16]

Faith-Forming-in-Consciousness Cuisine : "The Move-ing Sermon"

As we approach David Buttrick's cooking station, he is busy getting plates out of the cabinet. A copy of his book *Homiletic: Moves and Structures* (1987) is prominently displayed. He is lecturing the crowd around his station about not serving a block of food on a single plate and calling that a meal. Buttrick commends replacing the static outline form of preaching with what he calls "moves," a series of "rhetorical units" or "language modules put together by some sort of logic. . . . Moves form in consciousness to pattern an understanding."[17]

As he talks he sets out several plates, end to end. Apparently each sermon requires several courses to lead the listener to an experience of satiety.

We step forward to hear his mellow yet decisive voice amid the din of the huge kitchen stadium hall. He is telling us that in preaching we are inviting listeners to imagine their individual stories with a new preamble, a new conclusion, and a new main character. We are inviting them to imagine that the focal point of their personal and social narratives is, not themselves, but Jesus Christ, for he is the focal point of God's story, the story of the church, a "being saved" community in the world.[18]

As he continues to talk, we form in our mind the thought that, just as a diner's appetite is satisfied as the meal moves from course to course, so the sermon listener's faith is formed in consciousness as the imagination, in a forward-moving dynamic, spurs one to visualize what is not yet by means of what is. In our multicourse dinner, we have to trust the cook as to what she has chosen. As listeners, we trust that the next course will flow from the one we're on now, but we don't quite know that our tomato mozzarella salad will be followed by lamb chops until the salad plate has been removed and the succulent chops are before us.

Buttrick pauses a moment and turns to the two cabinets behind him. One is marked "biblical metaphors," the other "cultural metaphors." He opens both cabinets and pulls a couple of jars from each. He informs us that preachers need to bring biblical metaphors that express God's character and purposes toe-to-toe with cultural metaphors to form the faith of listeners. To illustrate his point, Buttrick gives examples of metaphors that biblical authors use to convey our restored relationship with God. The metaphors include Eden, Jerusalem the Holy City, the cross, being born again, the kingdom of God, the body of Christ, a royal priesthood, the family of God, and the sacraments.[19] Imagery with its visual impact "assists focus in consciousness."[20]

Buttrick believes that when a text is a narrative we ought to allow the sermon to follow the contours of the narrative, and when a text features vivid imagery we ought to allow the imagery to shape the sermon, and beware of importing contemporary examples that mix our metaphors.[21]

We notice a covered tray of sermon samples set out on a table near Buttrick's station and, next to it, a stack of cards containing sample recipes. Lifting the cover, we pick up a sample by its toothpick and take the accompanying recipe card with us for future reference.

Sermon Sample: "Up against the Powers That Be" (Ephesians 6:10–19)

Buttrick's first and last sentences in each "move" show us how the sermon flows in consciousness from one thought to another. Between the first and last sentences in each move, the thought is advanced, developed, and fleshed out with illustrative examples.

After an initial setup in which he introduces the need for the strength of our faith, expressed in the military metaphor of the text, in the face of contemporary challenges, move 1 begins in this way:

First sentence: "Well, if you're going to live for God in the twentieth century, you're in for a fight." Last sentences: "Principalities and powers: the real enemy is unseen and bigger than we know. Listen, if you want to live for God in the twentieth century, you're in for a fight."

> Move 2: First sentences: "Now it's time to be honest. Our cause, the Christian cause, is absolutely hopeless." Last sentences: "God's world doesn't end with a whimper, but with choiring angels and the Lamb upon the throne. God's cause will be!"
>
> Move 3: First sentence: "Well, meanwhile back here on the battlefield, how do we fight?" Last sentences: "Listen, all you need tucked in your arsenal is a word. 'The Prince of Darkness grim, we'll tremble not for him, one little word will slay him.' Dear friends, the Word is Jesus Christ. There is no other word worth speaking. The Word is Jesus Christ."[22]

Faith-Forming-in-Consciousness Cuisine: The "Imagine That" Sermon

As we approach Richard Eslinger's cooking station, we see that he has David Buttrick's *Homiletic: Moves and Structures* out on the counter, as well as his own *Narrative Imagination: Preaching the Worlds That Shape Us.*

As we join the group in front of his station, we smell a delicious, but hard-to-identify fragrance wafting from the oven. It is spicy and appealing, but we're not quite sure what it is, and we see no signs of ingredients on the counter that would give us a clue. We are about to ask, but Eslinger is beginning his culinary talk. By means of images, says Eslinger, we don't just see with the mind's eye. We also hear with the mind's ear, smell with the mind's nose, feel with the mind's muscles, and taste with the mind's tongue.[23]

The smells from the oven are almost more than we can stand. I have decided it is a cheese soufflé spiced with a hint of nutmeg. My mouth is watering. I begin imagining that I am placing my fork into it and eating a fluffy bite—light, yet satisfying—and I begin imagining how I would make it at home.

Eslinger's deep, pleasant voice breaks through my soufflé dreams. He explains that the imagination enables us to "imagine that" a certain state of affairs exists, and, further, to "imagine how" it might exist. Imagining how tends to involve the personal agency, the participation of the listener.[24] Eslinger urges preachers to build these workings of the imagination into our sermons: "imagining that" and "imagining how." The preaching of the prophets, including Jesus, invited listeners to imagine both that a different state of affairs exists (the day of the Lord; the kingdom of God) and how they might participate in that new reality.[25]

Eslinger then goes to the fridge and gets out a Tupperware container full of stories. He retrieves a stack of images from the bag they came in and reties it so the remaining ones don't dry out. He sets the stories and images on the counter, side by side. He recommends that we build our sermons on the interplay between these two ingredients, story and imagery. Both are products of the imagination. Pointing to the container of stories, he tells us that stories provide a home for images, while images can often provide a clue to the interpretation of stories. Images can itinerate from story to story, maintaining prior relationships when they move. They can come to frame our views of self and world, emerging as master images, still connected to their stories. The images involved in the sacraments of baptism and Holy Communion illustrate this. Narratives evoke images, and images evoke narratives.

Eslinger advocates variety in our use of images and story in our sermon recipes. Pointing to the container of stories, he says that sometimes the narrative plot will be preeminent. Pointing to the bag of images, he says that sometimes an image will be the organizing agent.[26]

As we move to our next station, we pick up a card with cooking tips for using images in sermons.

Point of View in Cooking with Images

Questions the preacher should ask when using an image in a sermon:
How wide a visual field am I showing listeners?

(Am I presenting the congregation with a wheat field in Kansas, or a display case in a museum?)

How deep a connection do I want listeners to have with this image? Do I want them to look at it from the surface? "The med students slip into the theater seats and look down on the surgery going on. They watch carefully. Dr. Green is an artist."

Or do I want them to experience it more deeply? "You are a surgical nurse. You look on carefully. The patient was your Sunday school teacher when you were really needing a friend."[27]

Remember, point of view is built into every image we present in our sermon recipes. The key is to understand what we're doing. Just as a recipe fails if it has too many conflicting flavors, so we should guard against asking listeners to shift points of view too often and too abruptly.[28]

Celebration Cuisine: "The Experiential Encounter Sermon"

We now approach the cooking station of Henry Mitchell, well-known African American homiletician. He has copies of two of his books, *Black*

Preaching: The Recovery of a Powerful Art (1990) and *Celebration and Experience in Preaching* (1990), open on the counter.

As he gathers bowls and spoons, he offers a culinary history. He tells us that "At no point did the African rhetorical tradition permit emphasis on abstractness." Even the professional philosophers of the Yorubas of Nigeria insisted that ideas be expressed in images that common people could visualize. The "African insistence on images and action, tales and pictures with meaning," says Mitchell, "is no figment of primitive imagination: It is a sophisticated principle of communication."[29] He reminds us that the master sermon chef Jesus taught in brief, provocative narratives (parables) and that "art is still . . . superior to argument for preaching purposes."[30]

Mitchell holds up a key ingredient, a biblical text. Holding it toward us for our inspection, he warns us that he is not going to extract its ideas and discard its form, imagery, characters, and plot. He wants us to realize that both kernel and shell are edible in this case, and that throwing away one ruins the other. Mitchell wants to retain the ingredient of reason in his sermon recipe. Holding it up by its stem, he reminds us that, in cooking, every ingredient has its purpose, and the purpose of reason is to provide internal coherence and intellectual integrity to our sermons. But, according to Mitchell, reason is not enough. If reason is our only sermonic ingredient, ideas are taught, but they are not always "caught," that is, appropriated by the whole person—emotions and intuition as well as intellect.

Sermons, says Chef Mitchell, need another ingredient besides reason. That ingredient is the imagination. He is convinced that sermon chefs, if they want to serve up sermons in which hearers experience a joyous encounter with God that changes their behavior, need to employ the flavor enhancer called imagination.

As he talks, we think about substances that enhance the flavor of a variety of foods: salt and sugar, for example. We remember that yeast extract can enhance the flavor of savory foods.

"The imagination is the ingredient that enhances the preacher's ability to visualize the scriptural event in concrete terms that are parallel to hearers' current experiences. It enables her to read the Bible as if she were present in the stories read."[31] That experience of recognition is known as identification, and the imagination is what enables it to happen.

The preacher's recognition of one's own feelings and situations and actions in those of the character and plot allows her to create a sermon in which listeners can do the same, and be drawn into a vicarious experiential encounter. In that encounter the "tapes," or intuitive assumptions they've grown up with, which are not always positive, are replaced by positive biblical affirmations.[32]

To do justice to this approach, the preacher first encounters biblical truth with his whole personhood, because he identifies with the details, the action, and the personalities of the people in the text. Then he is able, not just to retell the story or text, but to relive it as he recounts it. That reliving involves pictures and images and plot. In that reliving, hearers encounter and experience it vicariously. They "see" issues more clearly because they are conveyed by means of pictures and plots. Ideas are not just taught, they are caught; that is, they are appropriated by the whole person of the listener through the dynamic of identification, which is a function of the imagination.

The flow of the sermon should not be designed to get a point across, says Mitchell, but as "a flow in consciousness which will be used to beget trust and change behavior."[33] His use of the term "consciousness" owes a debt to the work of David Buttrick (*Homiletic: Moves and Structures* [1987]), but the flow itself is patterned after the emotional logic of African American preaching. That flow is problem, complication, resolution, and celebration. Celebration is the emotional finale of the sermon. Not only narratives, but other genres of biblical literature are well suited to this sermonic flow. Mitchell calls them "vehicles of experiential encounter." They are the narrative, the character sketch, the group study, the dialogue, the monologue or testimony, metaphors, similes and analogs, and the stream of consciousness. Whatever our text, says Mitchell, preaching should use concrete images, familiar language, and familiar details.[34]

A tray of sermon samples tempts us in front of Mitchell's station. We pick one out to sample. It's a recipe for Mitchell's sermon on Luke 24:10[35] ("It was Mary Magdalene, Joanna, and Mary the mother of James, and the other women with them who told this to the apostles").

In this sermon, Mitchell taps into the differing conditions of his listeners. Some are downcast or resentful because their service is unrecognized. Others avoid ministry because it doesn't lead to grand rewards. He addresses people in both places with the example of "The Other Women," who, although nameless, were entrusted with the gift of being the first to announce the resurrection. Thus encouraged by his naming of our condition and God's response, we are to join in Mitchell's celebration of the "other women," what they have done for us, and what we might do for others if we follow their example.

We pick up the recipe card to take with us in case we want to make a similar recipe with another text in our own homiletical kitchens.

Sermon Sample: "The Other Women"

The first half of the sermon is fueled by questions with intervening reflection and commentary. (Page references are to Mitchell, *Celebration and Experience in Preaching*.)

> "Who in the world *are* these women?" (128)
> "Now what in heaven's name are they doing together?"(128)
> "Why are only three of them named and the others are not?" (129)

Then the sermon transitions to declarative statements that name the women's motives and their ministry.

Although they knew touching the dead would defile them, "Their gratitude and human sensitivity would not let them leave the job until it was properly and compassionately completed" (130).

Mitchell challenges his listeners to imitate the devotion of "the other women," but cautioning them that they, likewise, may well receive no rewards or recognition. He lifts up his own mother as a church missionary-social worker during World War I. He points out that God rewarded the "other women" with "the quiet honor and glorious joy of being first to tell the news that Christ is risen" (131).

Then the celebration ending:

> It was Mary Magdalene, and Joanna, and Mary the mother of James, and all those other women who were with them that told the news to the apostles. And we are compassed about with a host of still other women without name—mothers and grandmothers and wives and sisters and daughters who still tell the news and live it out, to the glory of God and the help of us all. Thank God for every last one of them! Praise God for that nameless host and for their valiant ministries! Amen! Amen! (131)

Celebration Cuisine: The "Erase-It-and-Replace-It Sermon"

We approach the cooking station of preacher and teacher Frank A. Thomas. On his kitchen counter are copies of both of Mitchell's books, as well as his own, *They Like to Never Quit Praisin' God: The Role of Celebration in Preaching* (1997). As we walk up, he is setting aside a bowl of discarded scraps to put down the disposal. It contains scraps of sermons that appeal to the rational and the cognitive, but don't reach the emotions and the will.

In front of us on the central counter, Thomas has several ripe avocados. He is busy carefully halving them and removing the large but inedible seeds. The rich, green halves of avocado he places on a platter, the inedible seeds he places in the garbage can. As he works, he is advising preachers to be attentive to their people's "core beliefs." Like Mitchell, Thomas identifies core beliefs as the intuitively held assumptions about God, life, and self that reside in hearers' psyches. Again, like Mitchell, he compares the core beliefs to tapes recorded from our childhood experiences and asserts that they are often negative. Examples would be "God is not trustworthy," "I am worthless."

As he talks, he is mixing crabmeat, grated cheese, spices, and breadcrumbs in a small bowl. After we have identified our people's deeply held, often negative core beliefs, Thomas advises us to preach to reverse or replace them with the gospel. He reminds us that we must open ourselves to an experiential encounter with the good news that reverses our own core belief(s) if we hope to connect with our listeners. We watch his hands deftly filling the luscious avocado halves with the succulent crabmeat mixture. He wants us to make "reversal," the contradiction of negative core beliefs, the central dynamic of our preaching. We are to plan our sermons so that they culminate in this replacement or reversal in a moment of decisive celebration. Thomas defines that moment as a "release of imaginative capacity," in which "the remembrance of a redemptive past and the conviction of a liberated future transform the events immediately experienced."[36]

It has been a long time since breakfast, and we are having trouble concentrating on what he is saying, busy imagining biting into the avocado and crabmeat combo, and the burst of taste sensation we would experience, followed by energy that comes when we refuel our bodies with wholesome, filling food. As we refocus on Thomas's culinary talk, he sums things up: he tells us that behavioral change is the goal of the sermon. This release of imaginative capacity, this ability for us to envision ourselves and our futures from God's perspective, is directed toward change in our actions.

We are so hungry we can hardly stand it now, so we reach out and take a sermon sample from the tray in front of Thomas. He smiles encouragingly at us and indicates that we are welcome to taste the sermon recipe.

"Sin Is Crouching at Your Door" (Genesis 4:1–16)[37]

We are people who live with sin crouching at our door.

For Cain, as for us, it is like a panther, closing in for the kill.

For Cain, as for us, sin is the temptation to lie to ourselves and to God about our motives.

When we do this, we are at Satan's mercy.

The power of sin is broken when we tell the truth. To God, to a trusted friend. But we need to tell the truth.

We can then embrace our identity as truth tellers who have been forgiven of our sins by Christ and his life and death for us.

We start to move on to the next station, but Thomas tells us to wait a moment. There is an ingredient he hasn't talked much about that is absolutely essential to his sermonic cuisine. It is the imagination, a key ingredient of experiential preaching, preaching that stimulates the senses—a stimulation that stirs identification, emotion, and interest. That is what ultimately influences, not just the intellect, but also the behavior.[38]

At the heart of experiential preaching is the use of metaphorical language laden with sense-arousing images.[39] The Bible is filled with descriptive, imaginative, metaphorical language and images that stimulate the senses. "Life is full of sense-appealing 'usable shapes' that can be carved into images that vividly connect with the sense of the listeners and help people experience fresh encounter." Thomas encourages preachers to work hard, attentive to both text and life, to develop the knack of metaphorical language, which he calls "chiseling things into 'usable shapes.'"[40]

Imagination is key to the moment of celebration, "the experiential assurance of Grace that overcomes evil."[41] By the exercise of the imagination, the preacher identifies and fashions affirmative images (from text or life) that strike people in their inner core, and the Holy Spirit utilizes the images to help the hearer experience the transforming and liberating power of the gospel.[42]

Cinematic Cuisine: "The Four Pages Sermon"

We approach the cooking station of teacher of preaching Paul Scott Wilson. His 1999 book, *The Four Pages of the Sermon: A Guide to Biblical Preaching,* is on the shelf behind him. We learn the reason as he begins talking: his culinary methods are so clear-cut and memorable that he doesn't need to refer to a cookbook.

Today Chef Wilson is preparing sweet-and-sour pork over rice. He talks as he works, placing morsels of pork speared with decorative toothpicks on a tray for sampling. He explains that he has devised a detailed, yet clear methodology for forming sermons that honor both imagination and reason. He presents "two essential, interrelated metaphors for the preaching task, making movies and composing discrete pages of a sermon."[43] The four pages are theological functions that the preacher sets in motion in crafting the sermon, and they also become components of the sermon. Wilson offers them as tools for crafting and analyzing our sermons. The four pages are trouble in the Bible, trouble in the world, grace in the Bible, and grace in the world.

He searches the cabinet for vinegar as he explains the "trouble" pages of the sermon. Trouble is the theological problem that gave rise to the biblical text or the manifestation of sin in either the Bible or the world. He searches the cabinet for honey as he explains the "grace" pages of the sermon. "Grace" refers to the actions of God, unconditionally loving, covenant-creating and restoring, as well as overcoming human sin in the world of the Bible and today.[44]

He suggests that preachers think of themselves as filming their sermons, using the metaphor of moviemaking to teach preachers how to incorporate visual, sensory detail into their sermons, and to use plot and imagery to fuel the sermon's forward-moving energy. The metaphor of the four pages, which can be ordered in various ways, ensures theological balance and integrity in the sermon. Wilson gives specific advice on "filming trouble in the Bible," "filming trouble in the world," "filming grace in the Bible," and "filming grace in the world."

Chef Wilson includes a number of specific culinary methods for shaping sermon recipes that listeners will savor with their imaginations.

- Use sensory language reflecting all five senses.
- Place scholarly and exegetical material within the story: have a character say it. Have some detail in the setting or action communicate it.
- Focus on small details of gestures of characters or objects to give clues to characters and relationships. Be as visual and sensory with biblical portions of the sermon as you are with describing current events and stories.[45]

- Create scenes and stories, don't just report them. This approach is
  a variation on the novelist's dictum, "show, don't tell." This strategy could involve the portrayal of geographical setting with the
  aid of a Bible atlas, filming the story from the perspective of an
  often overlooked character, or placing the events and characters in
  a contemporary setting. For example, in a sermon on the Joseph
  cycle, Wilson places the Joseph story in Cape Cod in a Roman
  Catholic family of eleven sons.[46]

We know as we leave that we will hold this clear method in our minds
and will want to explore its nuances in greater detail. As we move on, we
lift a succulent morsel of pork from the tray by its toothpick, savoring the
mingling of aromas and flavors. For good measure, we also take a recipe
card along with us to add to our growing collection.

Futile Acts of Faith: Mary Anoints Jesus (John 12:1–8)

Page 1: Mary's sorrow at Jesus' impending death and her desire to
save him.

Page 2: Our sense of futility over whether our efforts can alleviate
anyone else's suffering.

Page 3: We marvel at the extravagant gesture made by both
Mary and Jesus, and while we don't understand them, we find hope
in them.

Page 4: Our seemingly futile efforts in ministry are extravagant
acts, an offering of our lives to God and our neighbor that have the
aroma of Christ and the power of God's love. [47]

Contextual Cuisine: The "Seriously Imaginable" Sermon

We approach the cooking station of preacher and teacher Nora Tubbs
Tisdale. A copy of her 1996 book *Preaching as Local Theology and Folk Art*
lies on the counter, so covered in flour and spices we can hardly read the
title. She has both ovens heating up and all kinds of ingredients spread
out on the counters. Sticks of unsalted butter are set out next to a tub of
low-fat margarine set out next to a can of Pam cooking spray. An egg
crate with extra-large brown eggs sits next to a carton of Eggbeaters.
Three packages of bacon sit in a row: regular, turkey, and tofu. Four
cartons sit side-by-side: fat-free half-and-half, heavy cream, skim milk,

and soy milk. There is a bowl of chopped onions mixed with chopped red bell peppers. A small bowl of sugar sits next to several packets of Splenda.

In front of her are five big mixing bowls and five eight-inch-square casserole dishes. In front of each is a recipe card. In her clear, pleasant voice, she is telling us that she is making several versions of a classic southern recipe: Virginia sweet corn pudding. Judging from the variety of ingredients, we decide she must be making a lactose-intolerant version, a vegetarian version, a diabetic version, a low-fat version, and a high-fiber version.

As her hands are busy, she talks about her cooking methods. She tells us that, while a number of preachers have advocated attentiveness to story, imagery, and metaphor in the biblical text, she believes that it is just as important to pay attention to those features in the congregational context. She considers preaching to be a form of "local theology" that has as its goal the transformation of the imaginations of the hearers in accordance with the message of the gospel.[48] That means, she tells us as she sprays Pam into one casserole dish and spreads a light layer of butter in another, that the preacher's primary task is to put his or her own imagination to work brokering a link between Scripture and congregation, appealing to the imaginations of the hearers through the images of Scripture.[49]

Cultural exegesis, according to Tisdale, involves attentiveness to key people, people on the margins, key events past and present, rituals, architecture and visual arts, and events and activities in the church's life. It also involves exploration of congregational identity through key myths or stories, both from its own past or from such sources as fairy tales, biblical stories, epic novels, movies, songs, and Greek mythology.[50]

The theology expressed in our sermons should be intelligible and capable of reasoned defense, grounded in Scripture and church tradition, and "seriously imaginable" for culturally conditioned people. "Like a three-legged stool," says Tisdale, "preaching teeters precariously if any one of these foundations is neglected."[51]

As she mixes up a thick, yellow batter in each of the five bowls, she explains that her focus is on the third criterion: being seriously imaginable. "It is not enough to speak of the presence of God and the forms of life appropriate in God's presence in terms that can be imagined in fantasy, yet cannot be envisioned as real possibilities for real people in their real social world. Theology should be formed in such a way that people from out of the midst of their own sociocultural location can affirm, 'Yes, we can envision that as a real possibility for us.'"[52]

Tisdale proposes five different recipes for bringing text and context together in transformative ways, using story and imagery. She points us toward a small table on which the cards are spread out and turns back to her task, donning hot mitts to put each casserole pan in the oven.

Recipe #1

Preaching can affirm and confirm the right imaginings of the congregation. Tisdale cites as an example a pastor who preached on Matthew 15:21–28 (Jesus and the Canaanite woman) who told the story of stone soup—about three hungry soldiers on their way home from battle who stop in a village and ask for food. Scared, suspicious townspeople hide their food. So the soldiers announce they'll make their specialty, stone soup. They take a large pot, fill it with water, place it over an open fire, and add the "magic ingredient": three smooth stones. All afternoon they stir it, stopping to taste it and comment on what would make it better. At each suggestion, one of the townspeople contributes the needed ingredient until the entire town turns out to feast on the best soup they've ever eaten. Next to this story, the preacher told three specific stories of how his congregation had made stone soup, combining talents and compassion to help others throughout the years.[53]

Recipe #2

Preaching can stretch the limits of the congregational imagination. Tisdale gives the example of a young pastor who preached on Ephesians. She began with a vivid picture of how we define family (those we know), picturing blood relatives and close friends around a table, then broadened this out to how God defines family (those who are known by God), and had the congregation picture a greatly expanded table fellowship.[54]

Recipe #3

Preaching can invert the assumed ordering of the imagined world of the congregation. Tisdale recounts a sermon she heard on July 4, 1976, on Luke 20, "Render unto Caesar." The preacher began by having the congregation imagine a coin on which was stamped Caesar's image. He talked about the blessings of life in America and positive points in our history. He then asked the congregation to imagine themselves stamped with the image of God and fleshed out areas in which demands of Caesar and demands of God might conflict and in which we as Christians are not to place any sovereign above God.[55]

Recipe #4

Preaching can challenge and judge the false imaginings of the congregational heart. Tisdale cites a sermon preached by Allan Boesak during apartheid in South Africa called "The Reuben Option." It began with the story of Joseph's brothers who wanted to kill him, and his brother Reuben who came up with the "respectable compromise" of not killing him but of selling him into slavery. Boesak placed next to this the story of Kaj Munk, a Danish pastor who was executed by the Nazis for his anti-Hitler stance. Boesak encouraged his listeners to take on a "holy rage," remembering that "the signs of the Christian church have always been the lion, the lamb, the dove and the fish. But *never* the chameleon."[56]

Recipe #5

Preaching can help congregations imagine worlds they have not yet seen or even imagined. Tisdale cites Walter Brueggemann's notion that "the purpose of the sermon is to provide a world in which the congregation can live." Preaching functions as a double dynamic, of prophetic criticizing and prophetic energizing. Preaching as local theology, says Tisdale, also offers them a world to *live into*. The best-loved example of such a strategy is Martin Luther King Jr.'s "I Have a Dream" speech, with its power to "create a world this nation as yet could only imagine—but a world for which many hungered and yearned." He "gave us a world to live into." It is like the sermon recipe advocated by Walter Brueggemann: images of fear and terror are supplanted by images of hope.[57]

Contextual Cuisine: The "Key Metaphor" Sermon

We approach the cooking station of Justo L. González and Pablo A. Jiménez, authors of *Pulpito: An Introduction to Hispanic Preaching*. A variety of delicious smells wafts toward us, drawing us toward their kitchen.

We know that Tex-Mex and Cal-Mex cooking, with its limited ingredients, is not representative of the richness and variety of Mexican and Hispanic cuisine. The array of ingredients spread out on this counter confirms that. Here we see far more than the beans, cheese, flour tortillas, and chips and salsa we may be used to. This station offers a gorgeous array of poblano peppers, corn husks, squares of bitter chocolate, slivered almonds, green pepper, raisins, oranges, queso blanco, piles of spices, ripe tomatoes, onions, eggs, and corn flour. The oven is hot for baking the flan, the griddle is ready for the corn tortillas, and a mixture of broth, spices, and chocolate bubbles on the stove ready to be poured over succulent pieces of chicken. A whole array of recipes is possible from these ingredients.

What to choose to serve to what congregation? Jimenéz and González talk with us about their culinary methods as they work in the kitchen. They tell us that the imagination has a key role in guiding biblical interpretation and shaping the sermon. A central dynamic in this process is the discernment of key metaphors that connect the social relations that shaped the biblical text and those that shape Latinos/as' experiences today.[58] Jiménez picks up a copy of his colleague Justo González's book *Santa Biblia: The Bible through Hispanic Eyes*. He tells us that in that book, Gonzalez identifies six key metaphors or "paradigmatic concepts" that Hispanic theologians and Latino/a pastors use in their writings and sermons to express the experience of Latinos/as in the United States. They are marginality, poverty, *mestizaje*, exile, alienness, and solidarity. Jiménez recommends that preachers use these metaphors to convey the correlations between the experiences of people in biblical texts and in Latino/a congregations.[59] Using this basic approach, preachers can be alert to any number of images or metaphors in biblical texts that can correlate experiences of biblical people and contemporary people.

We are pointed toward a table on which are recipe cards for a sermon on Luke's account of the birth of John the Baptist.

"Child of God" (Luke 1:57–66)

In this sermon, United Methodist Bishop Minerva Carcano focuses on the experience of the parents of John the Baptist as they anticipate his birth, insisting that he be named John, which means "The Lord has been gracious." She challenges listeners, like the parents of John the Baptist, prayerfully to consider the naming of children in their lives and in this country. If we truly believe in their identity as children of God, we will heed God's call to ensure that they are treated in a manner that fits their name.[60]

What a different way to view John the Baptist! Not as a fearsome prophet of repentance, but as a gentle baby whose birth is a miracle of great significance.

Zechariah and Elizabeth prayerfully considered the birth of their child, and Elizabeth insisted he be named John—the "Lord is gracious."

John's name signified that the day of the Lord's favor would arrive.

We need to stop and prayerfully consider the children being born in this country.

We say we love children in this country but do nothing in the face of their homelessness, poverty, deportation, abuse, and prostitution.

Bishop Carcano gives examples of several children she knows struggling to make their way, sometimes aided by the church, struggling for hope.

John, Lauralee, Oscar, Mayra.

What's in a name? Everything, if that name happens to be "Child of God."

Conflict-Resolution Cuisine: The "Sudden Shift" Sermon

We follow the sounds of a beautiful piano rendition of "Jesus Loves Me" to the cooking station of Eugene Lowry, jazz pianist and teacher of preaching. A grand piano takes up most of the kitchen, and he is currently sitting at it rather than cooking behind the counter. As he plays, he talks about his theory of sermon shaping. He tells us that in his 1980 book *The Homiletical Plot* he put forth his belief that sermons, rather than announcing conclusions at the outset, should be driven by the dynamic of anticipation.

Lowry asserts that Charles Rice's story sermon, Fred Craddock's inductive sermon, Henry Mitchell's celebration sermon, David Buttrick's "moves" sermon, and his own "Homiletical Plot" sermon have this in common: they don't announce the preacher's conclusion at the outset. They keep the cat in the bag until the end.[61]

This, he reminds us—as he increases the volume from pianissimo to mezzo forte—was his homiletical plot, a sequence of initial conflict, complication, reversal, and resolution. He ends with a flourish, and now he gets up from the piano and comes to the kitchen counter where he has assembled an array of ingredients.

On the counter he has placed a bottle of vegetable oil, a bowl of chopped onions, a couple stalks of celery, little spice boxes of dry mustard and celery seeds, a bottle of ketchup, a bottle of apple cider vinegar, a bottle of apple juice, Worcestershire sauce, and a jar of honey. Also a little pile of dark green seeds sits on a cutting board next to a rolling pin. On the stove is a saucepan with a wooden spoon standing by. What's all this for? I'm guessing some kind of sauce? Assembling of ingredients, simmering them and then . . . using them for . . . ? I guess we'll find out.

He takes up a rolling pin and begins rolling it across the pile of little green seeds. A sweet aroma drifts toward us as the rolling pin breaks them up, and we recognize the smell of anise seeds.

As he crushes the little seeds with the pin, Lowry is telling us that he has developed the homiletical plot into a full-blown text-to-sermon method. He labels his three-part process attending, imagining, and shaping.

"Attending" involves immersing oneself in the text, looking for trouble and positioning oneself to be surprised.

He pauses in his talk for a few moments as he heats vegetable oil in a saucepan, stirs in chopped onion and celery, and begins stirring.

He goes on, explaining that "imagining" involves naming important issues, images, and incidents; ruminating potential connections; and consulting the commentaries as scholars in residence.

He pauses, now adding to the pan (one ingredient at a time, with periods of stirring in between) the anise seeds, celery seeds, dry mustard, ketchup, chili sauce, apple juice, apple cider vinegar, Worcestershire sauce, and honey. He stirs slowly as the ingredients dissolve and interact. He'll be stirring for a while. Kansas City steak sauce takes its time in thickening.

Lowry continues, telling us that shaping involves naming the sermon focus and strategy, recognizing the sudden shift and positioning the good news, planning the sermon process, and naming the aim.[62]

With regard to shaping the sermon, Lowry, citing David Schlafer's *Surviving the Sermon*, specifies three means—image, story, and argument—by which a sermon can be unified, by which its contents can be carried through the stages of its plot. Schlafer advises preachers consciously to integrate the voices of Scripture, congregation, culture, their own experience, and church tradition by means of an image, story, or argument and to use that as the forward-moving dynamic of the sermon. Such sermons have an excellent chance of becoming sacraments of grace to those who hear them.[63]

Given the way Lowry understands the shaping or plotting of a sermon, it always involves a sudden shift, what Fred Craddock calls the "shock of recognition." When an image is the integrating factor of the sermon's plot, an image can be crucial to the reversal of the text, as the preacher shows a new import of the image or replaces one image with another.[64] Lowry gives the example of Jacob's limp (Gen. 32) as an image that captures the dramatic reversal in a sermon based on this text. For years Jacob has been running, but he has been a broken, fractured person. Now he is whole, whole enough to afford the slow, disjointed rhythm of a limped walk.[65] Lowry, drawing on the thought of Patricia Wilson-Kastner, distinguishes between images and imagery. Scriptures engage our senses and emotions directly by means of images. They invite us to enter as participants in stories—historical, fictional, and mythical. They confront us intellectually with arguments. Imagery is more than visual. It includes all the physical and sensory dimensions of the world portrayed in the sermon. Sometimes a single image from a text brings the whole sensory dimension into focus.[66]

Now Lowry is setting the thickened sauce aside to cool. He has a container set out to put it in the fridge where it can be kept up to a month, waiting for the right moment to be taken out, returned to room temperature, and brushed on a steak during the last twenty minutes of grilling. So into the fridge it goes, until the right steak comes along.

As we move to the next station, we take time to collect a recipe card to help us remember the method we'll try when we get home to our own kitchens.

"A Knowing Glimpse" (Luke 24:13–35)

Oops: Why are these two friends of Jesus leaving Jerusalem, where all the action is, where they've been told he may not be dead?

Ugh: Were they afraid they might be victims in this violence? Were they confused and just wanted a walk to clear their heads?

They are joined by a stranger. How can they not know who he is?

Aha: Lowry tells a story of friends of his, Tex and Peggy Sample, who invited him to a birthday party in Lowry's honor at their home. Peggy Sample, a fine artist, had painted a picture of Lowry as a clown and hung it over the mantle. He says he walked by it several times that night and didn't recognize his own face until Tex pointed it out to him.

It was too incredible to think Peggy had painted his likeness, so he didn't recognize himself.

Similarly, the disciples needed to have the identity of the stranger spelled out, because it was too incredible to imagine.

Whee: So Jesus took the bread, blessed it, and shared it. And as the bread was broken, so was the veil of their ignorance. It was a "knowing glimpse," the kind that takes the breath away, that grips the soul.

Yeah: And the good news gripped, not just their souls, but their bodies, too. The text tells us that within the hour, "They got up and returned to Jerusalem."

"That's the way it can be for us all. If any of us ever get a glimpse— you know, even just a fleeting, momentary, fragmentary glimpse— well, it'll turn you around! Yes, it will."[67]

Shape Your Sermon So That It Contains Gaps: Linda Clader's Voicing the Vision

We approach the cooking station of Linda Clader, Episcopal priest and homiletics professor, just as she is pouring what looks like waffle batter into a waffle iron. We watch the golden batter ooze into the heated waffle iron as she closes the lid. As it begins to cook, a delicious smell wafts toward the folding chairs on which we have taken a seat.

Chef Clader is telling us that imagination is closely linked in her mind to prophetic proclamation, preaching that challenges and reorients listeners. She tells us that "to the degree that we [preachers] identify ourselves as prophets, we are called to offer . . . the kind of slightly tilted or inside-out vision that can allow us to name the box and loosen its hinges."[68]

Speaking of a box with hinges, we are getting impatient to taste these waffles. There are several pitchers on the counter, and we begin to wonder what is in each. Warm golden gravy? Warm golden maple syrup? Blueberry syrup maybe? Is that whipped butter in that dish?

But Chef Clader is talking and we need to listen.

> Preaching with imagination has never been about simply decorating a sermon to seduce people into listening. . . . It has always been about allowing space for a kind of playful energy that can delight and surprise us out of the places where we are spiritually stuck, that can kindle and strengthen hope. It has always been about flinging open windows for the light of the Spirit; about setting doors ajar for God's holy Breath.[69]

Chef Clader turns to chapter 8 in her book *Voicing the Vision*, called "A Gift Loosely Wrapped." She offers concrete suggestions for shaking up the way we usually form our sermons to leave more room for listeners' imaginations to be at play. She believes that what holds a congregation's attention is the gaps between things, rather than overt exposition.[70]

Speaking of gaps between things, our minds are on waffles, indentations that soak up whatever we pour on them. We are weighing the merits of gravy versus syrup.

Meanwhile Chef Clader is advising us to look to movies and TV for lessons in maintaining suspense. She suggests that our sermons, like film, break away from the linear plot through a variety of strategies. One is flashbacks, sometimes offered as dream sequences or alternative story lines. She thinks transitions are overrated and suggests we try bringing in an apparently unrelated statement, scene, or story that causes the listeners to perk up and think, "Where is this going?"As she talks she lifts the lid of the waffle iron and gently pulls and pries the cooked waffle out and places it on a plate. Rather than cutting it along its neat, straight rows, she tears it into randomly sized pieces as she talks. She is telling us that we can place chunks of narrative next to one another without overdrawing the spaces between, and we can end our sermons abruptly, finishing off with a hint rather than a conclusion. She ends her talk by asserting that she has faith that listeners can hang in there, as long as they catch a hint that the sermon's current is steady and the goal is certain.[71]

She pushes the plate of waffle pieces toward us and indicates that we are to pick whichever toppings we like.

"Intervention" (Mark 2:1–12)

"Imagine it this way"—Dramatization of the paralytic in the second person: "Maybe you've been lying on this mat of yours for a long time." The sermon invites us to experience the man's situation and emotions and identify them with our own.

"But today something's up"—Dramatization, from the perspective of the paralytic, of what it feels like for several friends and family members to surround your mat, lift it, and carry it to the house where Jesus is, then lower you clumsily through the roof until you are once again lying on a floor looking up at their faces above you and Jesus' face and hearing his command, "Stand up."

"And you do stand"—Dramatization of feelings, physical and emotional, of the paralytic as those around him help him to stand. It concludes with the statement, "The hands of those friends were God's hands, too."

> *Have you been there?*—The sermon invites listeners to reexperience their own journeys from paralysis to healing through the lens of this text. It moves the listeners through stages of immobility, resistance, and the intervention of friends and family, in whom the preacher invites the listeners to recognize the presence and activity of God.[72]

Shape Your Sermon to "Serve a Richer Fare at the Table of the Lord": Post–Vatican II Sacramental Preaching

We come now to a group of people who are all engaged together in setting a table that contains both the Word and the bread and wine. They are homileticians from Roman Catholicism and other communions that practice the service of the Lord's Table on a weekly basis: Eastern Orthodoxy, the Anglican Communion, and the Disciples of Christ. They all share a sacramental view of preaching and a perspective in which Word and Table form two parts of a unified whole. They are the contributors to a recent book of essays titled *Homiletics at the Double Feast: Homiletics for Eucharistic Worship*.

Stephen Vincent Deleers, a teacher of preaching at St. Francis Seminary in Milwaukee, looks up from his work of placing the elements to provide us with some helpful background to this Table setting, informing us that the Second Vatican Council sought to increase awareness of the dignity and importance of the Sunday homily for Roman Catholicism. He adds, "Such veneration, such respect for the real presence of Christ in both Word and Sacrament, must be evident as we preach—just as evident as when we handle the Eucharistic bread and wine."[73]

Eastern Orthodox priest and homiletics professor J. Sergius Halvorsen is meanwhile nodding in agreement. He remarks that the Lord's Day liturgy for him is like a fine dinner party in which conversation, setting, and meal combine to form a complete and satisfying experience.[74] He adds that his tradition has not "made a sharp distinction between word and sacrament, never placing word and sacrament in opposition," instead viewing them as "one holistic 'eucharistic word.'"[75]

Two other contributors to *Homiletics at the Double Feast* are listening with interest. One is Mary Ann Wiesmann-Mills, O.P. She adds that a vital connection between preaching and Eucharist includes a call for poetic, imaginative preaching, in which preachers are poets, not moralists.[76] She cites Walter Brueggemann's affirmation that "The deep places in our lives—places of resistance and embrace—are not ultimately reached by instruction" but "only by stories, by images, metaphors, and phrases that line out the world differently, apart from our fear and hurt."[77]

Linda Clader has taken a break from her kitchen station to help set this table. She looks up from placing a plate and adds, "A sensory homiletical language . . . is entirely appropriate for the supremely 'materialistic' context of our sacramental liturgy. In fact, using a significant proportion of concrete imagery in our preaching may even help alert our listeners to the concreteness of the rite we are celebrating."[78]

Shape Your Sermon as a Homiletical Slide Show: Mike Graves, *The Fully Alive Preacher*

As we walk toward the next station, we see that Mike Graves, author of *The Fully Alive Preacher: Recovering from Homiletical Burnout*, is seated at his station, not cooking yet, but in the planning stages. He has cookbooks spread out around him, and on his laptop is a PowerPoint presentation he's making of the sequence of foods he will be serving. The food choices seem to build in deliciousness and intensity from start to finish, starting with a savory soup and building to a enticing entrée, followed by a flaming dessert.

He looks up from his planning to smile at us and to give a brief culinary address. In it, he suggests the term "episodic preaching" as an umbrella term encompassing both inductive and narrative preaching. Episodic preaching views the sermon as a series of vignettes stitched together in quiltlike fashion. Pointing to his laptop slideshow, he suggests we imagine a PowerPoint presentation. Some of the slides are exegetical, some are illustrative, and others deal with application. He suggests that we map our sermon. That is, we start with the sermon's destination, what some teachers of preaching call its focus or theme. Then we decide our sermon's starting point. Thus, "What comes last?" is the first question; the next question is "What should come first?" His advice is that we place the most moving portion of our sermon last and the second-most-moving portion first.[79] Not everyone agrees with him, he points out, but he cites Fred Craddock's claims that sometimes a sermon can start in "the shallow end," before inviting listeners into "deeper waters."[80]

Shape Your Sermon Like the Text: Genre-Shaped Preaching— Thomas G. Long, *Preaching and the Literary Forms of the Bible*

We approach the cooking station of Thomas G. Long. He has an array of fresh ingredients out on the counter, representing the whole biblical food pyramid. There are platters of juicy psalms, pungent proverbs with toothpicks in them, strings of freshly picked narratives, parables with the stems still on them, and a plate of epistles wrapped in parchment.

There are vegetables—not the shriveled kind that show signs of having been held against their will in the vegetable drawer for weeks—but yellow, orange, red, and green peppers, gleaming with vitality, and rustic carrots still with bits of dirt clinging to them from the digging. Every shade of green is represented as well, from shallots to broccoli. There are fruits—not brown bananas or spotty apples, but specimens at the perfect point of ripe but not rotten.

As we approach, Long has his back to us as he peers into an industrial-sized fridge. He emerges from its depths with a round of fresh, white, mealy cheese, a mozzarella baseball, and a shard of parmesan cheese so solid it looks like it could cut your hand. He places them on the counter as he begins his talk. He smiles warmly at us and suggests that we take a seat on one of the folding chairs, since this may take awhile.

We take a seat, and, while waiting for him to begin, notice several books spread out on the counter next to the shallots. There is a book on nutrition. There is a copy of *The Joy of Cooking*, its red ribbon marking the final chapter, "Know Your Ingredients." There is his own book, *Preaching and the Literary Forms of the Bible*. There is a copy of his *The Witness of Preaching* open to chapter 8, "Images and Experiences in Sermons."

He begins to give us the back story to his culinary approach. He tells us that, beginning in the early 1960s, biblical scholars and scholars of literature shone a spotlight on the literary features of texts. They helped preachers to see that we need to bring more than our intellect to a text and that we need to regard texts, not just as vessels for ideas, but as genres of communication that reach forward to affect the reader similarly to the way they once sought to affect listeners.[81]

We look around the cooking station and notice both what is there and what is not. There are no mallets for pounding cheap, tough cuts of beef to make them more tender, but there are succulent steaks sitting beside a grill. There are no big bags of fake grated cheese, no big blue box of salt, no container of MSG, no sticks of margarine waiting to be made into sauces to disguise bland foods. There are no cans of creamed soup, whether chicken, celery, or mushroom. There are a few bottles of wine, a plate of lemon wedges, and sheaves of fresh herbs, cilantro, parsley, and basil.

Long tells us that his book on preaching and literary forms introduced an approach to shaping sermons based on the premise that texts, rather than packages containing ideas, are dynamic means of communication that come in a variety of genres: psalms, proverbs, narratives, parables, and epistles.

He lists the sequence of his cooking method for preparing sermons on various genres. It takes the form of five guiding questions.

1. What is the genre of the text?
2. What is the rhetorical function of this genre?
3. What literary devices does this genre use to achieve its rhetorical effect?
4. How in particular does the text under consideration, in its own literary setting, embody the characteristics and dynamics described in the previous question?
5. How may the sermon, in a new setting, say and do what the text says and does in its setting?[82]

As we move to the next station, we stop to collect a recipe card. This one's main ingredient is a proverb.

"Better is a dinner of herbs where love is than a fatted ox and hatred with it" (Prov. 15:17)

Picture in your mind's eye a humble table and a wealthy one.

Think back in your memory to various meals. Long remembers a meal when he was a seminary student guest in a country church. A man and his wife invited him home to dinner. The meal was simple, but the hospitality was warm.

He recounts a poignant story from Garrison Keillor's *Lake Wobegon Days* about how Keillor was assigned a home near the school to go to in case of a winter blizzard. Keillor's was a kindly, elderly couple, the Kloeckls. The story tells of their joy in greeting him, calling him "the storm child," and serving him oatmeal cookies and hot chocolate.

Long tells the story of a man who felt the communion of saints present with him when he took Communion. He then encourages us to brainstorm future meals at which we are attuned to the gracious presence of God.[83]

Contemporary Worship Cuisine: "Visual Interaction"

We now make our way to the cooking station of Joseph Webb.

Before we get to Dr. Webb's station, we pass by a television reporter with a camera crew from the local station. We stand nearby to hear the reporter's commentary.

"I'm food critic A. P. Tizer, on site at this year's Sermon Chefs Cooking Convention. Over the past twenty years or so, new worship forms characterized by popular music styles, informality of dress, and a focus on praise in music and prayers have sprung up in churches around the country and world. I'm standing here next to the cooking station of Sermon Chef Joseph M. Webb, author of *Preaching without Notes* (2001) and *Preaching for the Contemporary Service* (2006). Let's listen in on the sermon advice he's serving up."

As we approach Dr. Webb's station, he begins speaking, with a laid-back brand of eloquence, stating that preaching in contemporary worship needs to help people experience Scripture firsthand, rather than through a detached analysis of its theological, doctrinal meaning.[84] Preaching in contemporary worship needs to be interactive rather than passive, addressing the whole person, not just the intellect.[85]

Now he brings out a huge platter from under the counter and places it in the center of the counter. There is a mingling of food fragrances, their separate strands weaving together, appealing but undefinable. It is a platter heaped high with stories. They are hanging off the sides, dripping and gleaming, steaming and fragrant. He says he favors story as the mainstay of preaching in contemporary worship. He suggests that preachers become systematic collectors of stories from both life and the Bible. Holding up a story to the light, Webb advises preachers to tell stories in a way that is highly visual, using vivid details to bring the stories alive and invite listener participation. Stories teach, inspire, entertain, and shape behavior. They create visions—that is, they help listeners imagine a future by conjuring up what could be or will be, if we embody the positive vision of the text.[86]

Now he brings out several smaller plates and places them in a circle around the central story platter. He places a small card in front of each that identifies its contents: Points of Crisis, Relationships, Intersections of Characters' Lives, Minor Characters, Behind the Scenes, and Central Metaphors.

Webb now invites us to taste the contents of each platter. He advises us to look for points of crisis, points where people find themselves up against a wall and must figure out a way to get themselves or someone else out of a jam. In telling biblical stories, our goal is not to celebrate the heroism of the men and women of the Bible, but to depict their relationships with God and the people around them. Look for moments or points at which the lives of two or more people intersect, moments when the decision of one affects others. Tell stories of minor characters (whom he baptizes "Jethro" characters, a reference to Moses' father-in-law), and tell about what is going on behind the scenes in biblical texts; there is always a story behind the story. Webb believes that today's listeners are fascinated by behind-the-scenes formats, as evidenced by the popularity of shows that depict how movies or music videos are made.[87]

Webb advises preachers to structure their sermon around a central metaphor, something to which the mind can attach itself. Metaphors are sometimes found, but they are often created by the imagination of the preacher in her world interacting with the text and its world. The metaphor ought to express the sermon's bottom line. Any sermon requires focus and clarity, a requirement that is amplified many times over in a sermon to be preached without notes.[88]

We notice for the first time that Webb has not referred to any talking points written on an index card. He seems to be speaking spontaneously, and yet he doesn't ramble, but speaks with energy and conciseness. Webb states that the dramatic form of improvisation, in which an actor takes to a stage noteless and keeps an audience engaged for up to an hour, is the genre that resonates most fully with preaching. Such preaching requires careful preparation and forethought, but is delivered without notes and connects with congregations by means of spontaneity, intimacy, and energy.[89]

There are no recipe cards to collect, so we move on.

Emerging Church Cuisine: Beautiful, Dialogical Potluck

As we move away from Dr. Webb's station, we pass another TV reporter recording her report for the evening news. "I'm Ahn Trey, here reporting on the annual Sermon Chefs Cooking Convention at the fairgrounds." She looks around her with a perplexed air. "I'm looking for the Emerging Church Cooking Station. I haven't been able to find it, but in the meantime, here is the background on that organization."

Behind her is a group of people sitting in a circle of chairs. They stop the lively conversation they are enjoying to grin at each other as they overhear Ahn's use of the word "organization." Then they start talking again. We are close enough to be able to squint and see their name tags, which identify them as Doug Pagitt, pastor, Solomon's Porch, Minneapolis, Minnesota; Karen Ward, abbess, the Church of the Apostles, Seattle, Washington; and Brian McLaren, pastor, Cedar Ridge Community Church, Spencerville, Maryland.

The reporter launches into her prepared speech:

> The emerging church movement refers to the proliferation of faith communities in our postmodern setting whose forms are nonhierarchical; whose values, in keeping with Jesus' teachings, are antimaterialistic and community centered; and whose worship is participatory and multisensory. Rather than a movement, many emerging church leaders prefer to think of their efforts as a conversation. Emerging churches are divergent, but have in common the belief that the church should shape its corporate life in accordance with the practices of the kingdom of God that Jesus inaugurated in his ministry. This leads to a community life that is critical of consumerism and radical individualism in American culture.[90]

In worship, emerging churches value creativity expressed, not just verbally, but through a full range of artistic forms.[91]

The reporter looks around once again, gets a desperate look on her face, and signs off.

As we walk closer to the circle of chairs, we overhear phrases. "It should be beautiful," says Brian McLaren. "And usually narrative in form. And conversational rather than analytical. And more about showing and listening than telling and convincing."[92] We edge closer to listen in on the conversation. We learn that McLaren was an English professor before entering the ministry. He calls for a new appreciation of the Bible's poetic language. "Make the sermon pointless!" is his tongue-in-cheek advice about the obsolescence of three points and a poem.[93] Our challenge, he believes, is to turn "the sermon experience into a spiritual practice. So we are not just giving information. We are creating a spiritual experience, and we are guiding people in a group meditation. So that it is not just about telling people what to do out there. It is letting something happen right here."[94]

As we surreptitiously listen in, we hear Doug Pagitt say, "I think it should literally be a dialogue. . . . I'm talking about both in the preparation and the presentation."

"And it should respect the spontaneity of the Spirit," says Karen Ward. She adds quickly, "And the cooking skills of everyone in the community should contribute to it."

It sounds like a beautiful, narrative, dialogical potluck. We're not surprised that there's no single cooking station representing emerging churches.

My feet are tired and my pockets can't hold any more recipe cards. It's time we went our separate ways. I thank you for spending time with me as we have heard the wise advice of fiction writers and teachers of preaching—on porches and park benches, and in home office spaces, studios, music rooms, and kitchens.

Until we meet again, I promise to tend and feed my imagination carefully, and I hope you'll do the same.

Chapter Six

Sermon Sampler

T his chapter consists of several sermons I've preached over the past several years, without benefit of the specific insights of this book. I invite you to read them critically and to note places where they express its principles and places where they fall short.

The text in bold print in the sermons is for my benefit in memorizing (internalizing) my manuscript before preaching it and are not usually spoken in the oral performance of the sermon.

"Getting What's Coming to You": Jacob's Struggle at Peniel
(Genesis 32:22–32)

Occasion: Graduation service for graduating seniors and their families, faculty, and staff at Perkins School of Theology, Southern Methodist University, Dallas, Texas, May 18, 2007.
Location: Perkins Chapel.

Our text tonight shows us a scene to remember. Jacob gets jumped! Who could forget it?[1]

(YouTube Footage)

Who can forget the image of Britney Spears driving her car with her baby, head lolling, on her lap under the steering wheel?

Who can forget the image of a drunk Mel Gibson, face contorted, spewing anti-Semitic rantings at the LAPD?

Or David Hasselhoff trying to eat a hamburger off the floor?

The CEO of American Airlines got stopped after a golf tournament and got a DUI, but there was no footage. He apologized and is still running the airline.

But as long as they stay up on YouTube to be played and replayed before our eyes—who can forget?

If these scenes show these celebrities at their worst, then maybe it's too bad they were preserved for posterity. But if they depict their typical behavior caught on tape, then if they lose their reputation or their job, maybe they got what's coming to them.

(Jacob's Footage)

I'm trying to break this to you gently, but I may as well just come out with it. Incriminating footage has surfaced recently regarding Jacob. Because of it, he has been asked to take a leave of absence and will not be graduating with you tomorrow. I read to you from the Perkins Catalogue page 24, "Fitness for Ministry," where it says this: "The presence of patterns of personal behavior tending to be seriously disabling to ministry can be grounds for the deferral of awarding a degree until such time as the disabling patterns are overcome."

We have sonogram footage of a disturbing heel-grabbing incident from which he gets his name Ja'akov (he grabs the heel).

We have footage that shows Jacob abusing his brother Esau, withholding food from him until he sells him his birthright for a bowl of lentil stew. This isn't stockroom footage—like when they do a story on obesity in America and show the midriffs of random people walking down the streets of Minneapolis. You can see his face and hear his voice.

We have footage of an incident in which, at the suggestion of his mother, he impersonates his brother Esau, putting on his clothes, placing the wooly skin of young lambs on his hands and neck. It's dark in the tent, but you can clearly see his face as he deceives his old, blind father.

This footage shows "patterns of personal behavior disabling to ministry."

It's all the more damning when put up on a split screen with the simultaneous behavior of God toward Jacob. We have footage of God blessing

Jacob in two nighttime scenes at Bethel in chapter 28 when he has first fled the wrath of Esau and in chapter 32 at Peniel by the River Jabok the night before he faces Esau after a twenty-year separation. God's face we cannot see, but God's voice we hear. Promising to Jacob as to his father Isaac and his mother Rebekah, his grandfather Abraham and his grandmother Sarah, "I will bless you with sons, land, and descendants." And a final all-important thread of blessing that is most prominent in the Jacob stories, "I will bless you with my presence." The Lord in chapter 28 stands beside him and says, "I will be with you. I will keep you wherever you go. I will not leave you."

This footage in chapter 28 shows Jacob doing one of the things he does best: naming places. "Surely the Lord is in this place—and I did not know it!" And he rose early and took his stone pillow and set it up as a *mazurah* (monument witness to the revelation of God there) and poured oil on it to consecrate it, and he called that place Bethel (the House of God).

Jacob was better at naming places than living by the names he'd given them. He didn't always live as if he realized "the Lord is in this place!"

It would be like if you served several churches in the course of your ministry: Trinity Church. Grace Church. Church of the Incarnation. Christ Church. Aldersgate Church. Church of the Resurrection.

And in each one on Sundays, your people gathered for worship asking, Where's our pastor? And then gathering at the window—oh, she's out there putting up a stone pillar and pouring oil over it and etching something into it. "Our Lady of Perpetual Discontent," or "A Place Not Worthy of My Gifts."

Jacob didn't always live as if the "Lord was in this place." He didn't always show "fitness for ministry." Instead, his life shows patterns of

> Pretending to be someone I'm not to achieve my goals
> Not asking, "Is this wrong?" but "Will I get caught?"
> Becoming defensive when offered constructive criticism

I saw Tracy Anne Allred, our Perkins Director of Student Services, in the halls the other day, and I said, "Tracy Anne, with all due respect, how did Jacob ever get admitted in the first place?"

"Well, Alyce, as you know, on page 16 of the Perkins Catalogue under 'Requirements for Admission,' the number-one requirement is serious-ness of purpose. And he certainly had that!"

That's true enough. If only it had been the right one! He was and is a man obsessed with getting what he felt he had coming to him, with grab-bing the blessing.

(Perkins Footage)

It's tough for you students to say good-bye to Jacob, that guy you always talked to as he stood in front of you in the lunch line. The guy you chatted with when you came into your church history class and he was already there, sitting in the seat closest to the electrical outlet plugging in his computer. It's tough for us professors to say good-bye to him, too. He was the student we could always count on to raise his hand and ask, "Will this be on the test?"

Oh, yeah, Jacob, you can count on it! Everything you learned in seminary, everything you are and have will be on the test!

Here I was trying, through a succession of brief scenes focusing on Jacob's behavior, to implicate us for similar contemporary behaviors.

(Jabok Footage)

While we're all sitting safely here, Jacob is on the brink of the biggest test of his life. His struggle with "the man" by the River Jabok when he finally gets what is coming to him. There is an eerie similarity between the words Jacob (heel grabber), Jabok River, and *ye'ebeq* (he wrestles). The wordplay is not lost on us.

Jacob is stepping from one large flat stone to the next across the narrowest, shallowest part of the River Jabok, marking his way back and forth, back and forth, by the light of the moon. He plants his feet firmly, clenches his hands, and watches as everyone and everything in his life grows smaller and smaller in the distance.

He is left alone. or God's not even here, so he thinks. He said his petitionary prayer last night. "Save me from Esau. But now I have to make it through this night alone." He's forgetting the divine promise and blessing of presence: "I will be with you." It's a spine-crawling feeling to think you're alone and realize you're not. Especially when an unknown adversary jumps on your back.

Jacob's not alone. We're here, his fellow students, his professors. We have empathy for his struggle. Seminary has seemed like a long wrestling match for us. We've struggled with patterns of behavior . . . wondered about our own fitness for ministry at times, struggled with family conflicts, illness, sorrow, and death that don't all decide to back off so we can get our theological educations.

We are here for you. Think of the combined expertise in this room, in biblical knowledge, pastoral care, general wisdom about life.

I picture the biblical scholars standing here, the pastoral care folks there, and those with general life wisdom over there.

We would jump in and help you, Jacob, but we might get hurt.

So we'll coach you instead. The biblical scholars—they look to be form critics (one of them is wearing a bow tie)—lend their aid by attempting to ascertain the identity of the assailant. "Jacob, we think this is a River Demon. Ancient lore held that rivers were guarded by patron demons who kept people from crossing them. But the good news is that they lose their power at the break of day. So hang in there, you only have five hours and forty-five minutes to go."

The pastoral care folks call out, "Jacob, we feel that this assailant is a metaphor that signifies your guilt over the past and your fear for the future. It may represent the future coming upon you, the poetic justice for your earlier moral lapses; sons fool you with an article of Joseph's clothing as you fooled your father with Esau's clothing. So what you need to do is to completely let go of your guilt over the past and your fear over facing Esau tomorrow. And the good news is that you only have four hours and thirty-five minutes left until daybreak."

The biblical folks chime in again. "Jacob, it may not be a River Demon, because they usually take the form of animals. And we taken a vote and we don't think it's God—because of the strong theme that you can't see the face of God and live. Also, some of us feel that the idea of God as robust adversary is disturbing. We would point out to you that elsewhere in Scripture God is depicted as a tender shepherd and a mother hen. Hang in there, you only have two hours to go."

Another group decides to read the inspirational poem "Footprints" to Jacob, but the grunts and groans of the strugglers makes it impossible for them to be heard, and they get the feeling they're annoying him.

The biblical folks pipe up one more time. "We've come to a decision, Jacob. We think it's not God, but an angelic emissary. In several other stories, beings referred to as 'men' are actually angels. Given the fact that this adversary has only to touch your hip to put you out of commission and that he assumes authority to give you a divine blessing, that is our conclusion."

But now, the land is getting lighter, the fight less frantic. We move closer—it seems safe now, and we want to hear what's going on. "Let me go, for the day is breaking," says the man. He touches Jacob's hip and puts it out of joint.

Jacob, "I will not let you go unless you bless me."

To claim the blessing you must make your confession. "What is your name?" asks the man, and we realize that what he is asking is, "What is your character? What kind of person are you?"

To claim the blessing you must be honest. "The one who grabs the heel," says Jacob.

Then you get what is coming to you. "Your new name is Israel," says the man, "the one who struggles with God."

"Please tell me your name," Jacob presses the man.

"Why is it that you ask my name?"

"Only receive the blessing."

He is gone, and we didn't even see him leave.

Let's let Jacob compose himself, brush the dirt off his cloak.

Meanwhile it's our job to call the match. Who won?

The angel

> Didn't reveal his own name
> Got Jacob to confess his identity—full disclosure, no more
>   pretending.

Jacob

> Finally got what is coming to him.
> Confirmation that tenacity is not all bad—Still standing at the end
>   of the match
> Had an intense and moving experience of the presence of God—
>   face-to-face
> Got a blessing—consisted of a new name, new direction for his
>   tenacity:
> The one who struggles with God or God struggles.

Who could ever forget this footage of the Jabok struggle?

Jacob could, apparently. In the very next scene he lies to Esau, telling him he'd follow him south to Seir and instead heading north to Succoth. The biography unfolds. He bears the blessing to the end of his life. It's not like a merit tuition scholarship God revokes if we don't maintain a 3.3 GPA. He bears it, but seems to bury it. It never seems to blossom from the depths of his life to bless others with its beauty and fragrance. Instead he blurs into the sidelines of the action as his sons grow up to dupe him as he duped his brother.

His pattern doesn't have to be ours. My prayer for you is that you will play this footage of the Jabok struggle over and over again in your mind throughout your ministry.

That, in every struggle, in every betwixt and between scene, you will rehearse and rerehearse its pattern of behavior empowering to ministry: the sequence of conversion and transformation.

> To seek out time alone with God.
> To answer God's question honestly: What is your character?
> Thereby opening your life to the blessing you don't have so much to
> go out and grasp as to recognize as you hold it in your hands.

And in every place you are sent, set up your pillar, pour oil on it, and etch into it these words: "Surely the Lord is in this place, and I do know it!"

"Wisdom in Person": Ode to a "Woman of Worth"
(Proverbs 31:10–31)

Occasion: Clergywomen's Day Apart for the Women Clergy of the Central Pennsylvania Annual Conference, United Methodist Church, June 5, 2006.
Location: Shepherdstown United Methodist Church, Shepherdstown, Pennsylvania.

I attended a North Texas Conference clergywomen luncheon last month. Some old friends. Some new faces. After lunch, a pastor stood up to speak. I'd never met her but knew she was an associate pastor at a church in Dallas. She led us in sharing joys and concerns and, in a very organized manner, charted out the group's activities for the rest of the summer. The group thanked her for helping them stay organized and, after a closing prayer, the thirty-odd women (I don't mean clergywomen are odd, I mean around thirty women) briskly went out to their cars, got in, fastened their seat belts, and drove off to the next thing. The church member expecting a visit at the hospital, the child waiting to be picked up at school, the young couple waiting to meet with you about their wedding back at church.

I stuck around and talked to a few women I hadn't met before, then gathered up my purse and some papers lying near it on the table and headed home to my home office to work on an article I was writing for a preaching journal.

Once home I was putting the papers on my desk, and my eye fell on the tablet on top.

It said, "Things to Do Week of May 14–21." I felt the familiar surge of adrenaline that the sight of a "things-to-do" list always brings to me. *I'm on it!* I thought to myself.

- E-mail contact information to Todd
- Call hotel in Atlanta
- Call George
- Resolve issue with faith partners (avoid repeat of last year)
- Check with Teresa about menu (ham not good)
- Check out fireworks with the fire chief (How close is too close?)

What contact information? Which Todd? I know three. Why am I calling the hotel in Atlanta? And which one? Who is George? What issue am I to resolve with the faith partners? What happened last year? Why is ham not good? I like ham. What does Teresa have against ham? Fireworks with fire chief? I hope this is related to the Fourth of July picnic and not a romantic metaphor.

Then my eye slid back up to the top of the page to a line I'd skipped in my first reading. It said "Jane's Things to Do Week of May 14–21." My adrenaline ebbed. I felt disappointed.

I called her and left a message: "Hi, Jane. This is Alyce McKenzie. I was at the clergywomen's luncheon and I picked up some of your papers by mistake. I have your things-to-do list. Here's my phone number. Call me if you need them back."

She called back ten minutes later. "You have my list. Thank God!"

"What's it worth to you?" I joked. You shouldn't joke with people you don't know. Since there was no laugh on the other end of the line, I continued, "I'm going to be driving right by your church tomorrow on my way to school. I can drop it off then."

"Not 'til tomorrow?" she asked, with a desperate edge to her voice. "What time?"

"Around 2." I said.

"Not 'til 2? Well, OK. That'll have to do. Thanks for calling me."

I sort of hated to drop off the list to Jane the next day. I had bonded with it. It was interesting. It contained areas of mystery that my own list lacks. Though for someone else, my list might be interesting.

- Make sure Matt returns Frankenstein.
- Put fall courses on blackboard.
- Finish woman at well and man by the pool.
- Get wood glue to fix highboy.
- Call shutter man.
- Call Mary to congratulate her.

Maybe we should all exchange lists. Maybe we should just throw out our lists.

Or maybe we should all just use the same list. That's what traditional interpretations of this text by male commentators have called this text from Proverbs 31. A list of things to do for the total woman (or as one woman commentator put it, "the totaled woman"). A clergywoman friend of mine said recently of Proverbs 31, "I hate that text! No human woman could live up to that. It's a guilt trip waiting to happen. If anyone reads it at my funeral I plan to haunt them!"

I guess it's good to have a plan for the future. But what about the meantime? What do we do with it now? Because no matter how many clergy wellness seminars you attend for continuing education credits, you know that, when it comes time for the charge conference reports, they want you to be the clergywoman of Proverbs 31. They want an account of how you seized responsibility for singlehandedly nourishing and energizing everyone in your world. It's what we do. Peggy Lee says it well, "Cause I'm a (clergy) woman, w-o-m-a-n."

My NRSV says "Ode to a Capable Wife," but the Hebrew is better rendered, "Ode to a Woman of Worth." If she were a pastor the list would read something like this:

"Woman of Worth's Things to Do List June 4–11"

- Provide food for entire congregation daily.
- Provide tasks, motivation, and energy for all church volunteers.
- Replace all burned-out lightbulbs in church facility and congregational homes.
- Consider a location for the new church building, raise funds, and take care of all the details with regard to its purchase.

- Go to Home Depot and local nursery and purchase all plants and flowers for landscaping the new building and plant them.
- Provide clothing, food, and jobs for the poor in the community around the church.
- Make clothes for everyone in the congregation based on which colors are most appropriate to everyone's complexion.
- Work out daily at least an hour to gain and maintain upper-body strength.
- Be on the top-ten best-dressed clergywomen of America's list every year.

If the traditional understandings of this text—as a description of the ideal woman—are right, then grab that list and go! Are you sure you have time to be here today? Today is like the yoga class I signed up for Thursday nights at 8 p.m. at a fitness center near my house. The yoga room is right next to the racquetball court. So while we're lying in "dead man's pose" on the floor deep breathing, listening to the instructor cooing in her calming voice, "This is your class. This is your hour. Leave all your worries and responsibilities at the door and listen to your body," meanwhile there is the sound of feet pounding and bodies slamming into the wall and grunts of exertion from the court next door. East meets West.

So maybe today is yoga class so you can get back on the court tomorrow, list in hand, to work even harder, more efficiently down your list of things to do to bring in God's kingdom this week.

But what if traditional interpretations are wrong and Proverbs 31 is not the ideal woman but someone else? What if my friend who is going to haunt anyone who reads this text at her funeral is right in saying, "No human woman could do all this"?

What if the woman of worth in this closing scene of Proverbs is Wisdom herself?

Recent studies of the text insist that it's not talking about a human woman at all, but another woman entirely. She is someone who has made several cameo appearances before in the book of Proverbs. She shows up in chapter 1 standing in the marketplace, calling the young and foolish onto the path of God's wisdom. She shows up in chapter 8, again calling the foolish to seek God's wisdom, and describing her role as a joyful helper with God in the creation of flora, fauna, Fred, and Wilma. She shows up in chapter 9; here she builds the household of Wisdom, and stands before her seven-pillared home inviting passersby to come and feast at her table. This is no maniacal, multitasking human mom, my friends. This is the wisdom of God, imaged in Proverbs as a Wise Woman, a prophetess.

Throughout the thirty chapters of Proverbs that lead up to this final poem, Wisdom is shown as inviting us into her household where she provides us with all the things mentioned in the final chapter: food, clothing, light, wisdom, shelter. All metaphors for divine nourishment and nurture. Doesn't she remind you of someone? Someone who said, "I am the Bread of Life. I am the Living Water. I am the light of the world. I am the Way, the truth, and the life?"

That's all I have of my notes from this sermon. Where would you recommend I go from here in speaking to this group of clergywomen seeking wisdom and rest the day before their annual conference begins?

"Filled with Fear": Exhortation to Trust in God
(Proverbs 3:5–7)

Occasion: Opening worship service for the Southeast Jurisdiction Gathering of District Superintendents of the United Methodist Church, January 10, 2005. The theme of the gathering was "Healthy Churches, Healthy Pastors," and the liturgical season was Epiphany.
Location: Epworth by the Sea, St. Simons Island, Georgia.

Gary's Story: Part One

I have a friend named Gary. Gary is a computer analyst in his mid-forties and he has been married and divorced twice, most recently about three years ago. For about a year he has been dating a wonderful woman at our church named Gina, also divorced and with an adorable seven-year-old daughter she is trying to get full custody of. Gary and Gina came to me last winter and asked if I would marry them at the end of April. Our counseling and wedding planning were going along fine until, along about mid-March, Gary began to develop a case of very cold feet. When he shared this with Gina, she did something a lot more mature than I might have. Instead of getting angry, she suggested he go away for a daylong retreat to be alone with God and himself, to get clear about things. Gary started driving with no particular destination. He ended up at a beautiful site near Lake Texoma.

He got out of his car and began to walk, to soothe his jangled nerves, to center his thoughts on God. He sat down on a bench that overlooked the lake. He tried to breathe more deeply, to unravel the knots in his stomach.

As he stared out at the lake, it became a sort of soul mirror. It came clear for him that there were three knots in his stomach, and each had a name. One of the knots was his *fear* that he would just keep repeating the same relationship mistakes. The second knot in his stomach was the fear of the *chaos and pain* that could come from the custody battle facing Linda. And the third knot in his stomach was maybe the hardest, knottiest of all: it was the fear that maybe *he was just not worthy* of another person's love and was destined to have to face his future alone.

Gary was focusing on his fears, naming the knots. Because fear and anxiety are not just emotional or mental. Fear is physical. That's why blood pressure goes up when anxiety/stress goes up. We fear things that are beyond our human power to predict and control, that are stronger than we are, that have the power to destroy us and all we love. That's what we fear.

Our Fears

As a new year begins, it's wise to find a quiet spot and get some focus on our fears; name the knots **(point to stomach)**.

Name your knots. Knots with names of people close to you you're worried about. Spouse. Parent. Child. Sibling. Knot named your marriage. Knots with various church names on them. Knot with your own name on it—your own health. A knot named "declining numbers," a knot named "terrorism," a knot named "Avian flu."

D.S. Role: Hail, O Fearless One

We all have fears. Of course, as church leaders, bishops, district superintendents, seminary professors, we're not supposed to talk about them. It's not on the agenda at meetings. Our job is to soothe other people's fears, solve other people's problems, be the lightning rod for the conflicts of entire congregations. They may as well write up a notice in the Sunday bulletin. "Notice to all codependents; all triangulators and experts at transference; come to church tomorrow night, 7:30 p.m., Fellowship Hall, bring all your grievances, all your deep frustrations, all your anxieties . . . because the D.S. will be here!"

Hail, O Fearless Ones!

I'm a professor of homiletics at a seminary. I teach, research, have administrative duties, attend meetings, have three children in varying stages of neediness, preach, lead workshops, etc., etc., have responsibilities at our local church. Sometimes I get tired of students telling me about how anxious they are about all they have to do. And why their exegesis will be a day late. I think to myself, *Maybe I'll show up for class this Thursday without a lecture and explain to them how busy I am and how I'm sorry because I know that they are paying for the course, but I was in Georgia preaching at a conference and that I then had a meeting this morning and an article due yesterday and my son's school conference last night.* Or maybe I'll just do what you and I do: show up without excuses and do our best in difficult situations. Maybe I'll take a cue from all of you and do that thing you do: listen to other people's fears and anxieties and then, on the drive home, deal with your own on your own.

Who is there to listen to the fears of the fearless ones?

The Fear of the Lord: Common (Mis)Definition

I was sitting in the passenger seat at a stoplight in Dallas over the Christmas break. My then twenty-one-year-old daughter Rebecca was driving. We had been moving furniture from her room at home to her apartment in Dallas. I seem to always be brought in for the heavy lifting assignments. The car in front of us had a bumper sticker on it that read, "The fear of the Lord is the beginning of wisdom" (Proverbs 1:7).

"I don't like that verse in the Bible about fearing God," Rebecca said. "I'm about to graduate from college. I have enough to be afraid of without having to be afraid of God, too!"

Most people have the same reaction. They hear the phrase "fear of the Lord" and they think, "fear of punishment." Whenever something bad happens to them, they think, "God is punishing me." The TV preachers didn't help—telling New Orleans that Katrina was God's punishment for their decadent lifestyle. Pat Robertson doesn't help. Telling Dover, Pennsylvania, to expect God to abandon them for believing in evolution. And now his most recent reading of the mind of God—asserting that

Ariel Sharon's stroke is God's punishment on a leader who would give part of the Holy Land to Palestinians.

It's like when, in the grocery store rags like the *Inquirer* and the *Globe*, they take pictures of two celebrities and paste them together and put a background behind them and a headline connecting them: I don't know, Dr. Phil and Vince Vaughan standing arm in arm in front of a space ship. Headline: "Why Us? We Were Abducted by Aliens." Pat Robertson takes God's face and pastes it next to the faces of flood victims and an ill elderly leader and says one caused the other. If I were God, I'd sue! What are we to conclude if Pat Robertson ever gets sick or dies?

Fear of the Lord: Bible Definition

Pat Robertson and the TV preachers need to have their heads examined, but they also need to have their eyes checked. Because they are apparently unable to read the book of Proverbs. It does not say repeatedly, the "fear of divine punishment is the beginning of wisdom." It says the fear of the Lord is the beginning of wisdom.

Our text for today: "Trust the Lord with all your heart . . . fear the Lord and turn away from evil."

Some would prefer to substitute the word "respect" for "fear." Respect the Lord. The respect of the Lord is the beginning of wisdom. Too bland. The Bible says "fear": a combination of awe, obedience, and ordinary fright. Moses and the Israelites at Sinai. Isaiah in the Temple. Psalmists and prophets exhort the people to fear God. In the Old Testament, God tells God's people not to fear the Canaanites, not to fear the Assyrians, because God is with them.

In the New Testament, angels tell Mary and the shepherds, "Fear not!" Jesus lifts people to their feet, healed, saying, "Do not be afraid." Jesus tells us not to fear human beings who can kill the body but not the soul, but to fear the One who can destroy both (Matt. 19:28; Luke 12:4).

Why fear? Because human beings are wired to fear, serve, obey something beyond ourselves. Bob Dylan hit the nail on the head in his 1979 song "You Gotta Serve Somebody": "Well, it may be the devil or it may be the Lord/But you're gonna have to serve somebody."

You're going to spend your life in fear, giving power to something beyond yourself, so make it the fear of the Lord. The Bible uses the word "fear" to alert us to the fact that when we enter into the presence of God, we enter into a presence that is beyond our human power to predict or control, that has the power to destroy us and all we love—but who intends good and only good for us, and has the power and the desire to destroy all our lesser fears. Fear God, but no one and nothing else. The fear of the Lord banishes lesser fears. To fear the Lord, says one Old Testament scholar, is a wholly appropriate response to entering into the presence of one who is wholly good, but from whose presence we know we will not emerge unchanged.

The heart of the story lies in Susan's early query of Mr. Beaver, whether Aslan is a safe lion. "Course he isn't safe," replies Mr. Beaver. "But he's good."

Aslan is not a nice pet who will coddle them with purring comfort, keeping them out of harm's way: "I'm longing to see Aslan," says Peter, "even if I do feel frightened when it comes to the point."

"God is the only comfort," Lewis writes in *Mere Christianity*. "He is also the supreme terror: the thing we most need and the thing we most hide from."

Says a commentator on Lewis, "God is our only hope of happiness. To be happy is not to wear a blinding smile, to be materially gratified, to be assured that everything will turn out well. Happiness, as the four Pevensie children learn, lies in surrendering oneself to the good and thus to Aslan."

Wouldn't it be amazing if we could, not just grasp this in our heads, but grasp it in our emotions and experience? That the path to spiritual health lies in our living by the fear of the Lord?

Have you read the book of Proverbs lately? How do you think the wise teachers who wrote these sayings knew they were true? "Like one who grabs a passing dog by the ears, so is one who meddles in the quarrel of another." You who spend your careers trying to get out of triangles people and churches try to put you in know that. "A soft answer turns away wrath, but a harsh word stirs up anger." Anyone who has ever avoided a marital quarrel by not saying what you were thinking, or started one by saying it, knows that. By experience. They knew their sayings were true because they had experienced them.

Now, what about, "The fear of the Lord is the beginning of wisdom"? How do you think the sages knew that? What about, "The fear of the Lord leads to life (or is life indeed); filled with it one rests secure (and suffers no harm)" (19:23). How about, "The fear of others lays a snare, but one who trusts in the Lord is secure" (29:25)? What of, "The fear of the Lord is a fountain of life, so that one may avoid the snares of death" (14:27)?

Nancy

Trust in the LORD with all your heart,
    and do not rely on your own insight.
In all your ways acknowledge God,
    and God will make straight your paths.
Do not be wise in your own eyes;
    fear the LORD and turn away from evil.
It will be a healing for your flesh
    and a refreshment for your body.
                                        (Prov. 3:5–8)

This is my friend Nancy's favorite text. She wears a wig now. Once a month she sits in her chemo chair with her Bible open in her lap, reading Proverbs 3:5–7. She knows that life is a continual struggle between lesser fears and the fear of the Lord that makes them obsolete. Between anxiety and assurance, panic and peace, terror and trust, soul sickness and spiritual health. The fear of the Lord is the fear to end all fears. She sits in her chair, in between readings, closing her eyes, feeling the fear of death drain from her body as the fear of the Lord fills her with peace and joy.

Paul

Paul sat in prison, blood crusted around his ankles from the shackles. Listening to the cries of fellows prisoners and the click of the latch on the door. They were coming, he just didn't know when.

> Rejoice in the Lord always; again I will say, Rejoice. . . . Do not worry about anything, but in everything by prayer and supplication with thanksgiving let your requests be made known to God. And the peace of God, which surpasses all understanding, will guard your hearts and your minds in Christ Jesus. (Phil. 4:4–7)

Jesus in the Garden

A man kneels in a garden, deep in prayer. And what words move on his lips?

The fear of pain is the beginning of wisdom?

The fear of death is the beginning of wisdom?

The fear of loss and failure is the beginning of wisdom?

The fear of the Lord is the beginning of wisdom. Not my will, but thine be done.

The Two Windows

When I was a little girl about four, I guess I used to kind of like sitting in church. I would face forward and look at things. Sometimes I'd draw. Then one morning I noticed the big stained-glass window at the back of the church. And I just couldn't face forward that day. I stood on my fat little legs and faced the back, gazing at the window as if mesmerized. On the left side was a depiction of a man kneeling, hands clasped in prayer, face raised to heaven, tears on his face, glinting red as the sun shone through them. On the right side was a depiction of a man standing up, in a white robe, a calm look on his face, a slight smile, hands calmly at his sides, some sort of little red spots in the middle of his hands and his feet, too. I couldn't tell if he was standing on something or in mid-air. I stared at the two windows the whole service. Finally, as the last hymn was wrapping up, I tugged on my mom's sleeve.

"What is it?" she asked, annoyed to be interrupted while singing.

"Why can't that happy man help that sad man?"

She smiled: "They are the same man."

Gary: Conclusion of Story

We left Gary sitting on a park bench, didn't we—his stomach in three knots of fear:

That he'd repeat his mistakes.

That the struggle to blend a new family would be too much for him.

That maybe he wasn't even worthy of someone else's love.

Gary says he heard rather than felt the words, "Let them go. You don't need them anymore. Let them go."

As he gazed out at the calm waters, three geese toddled up to him, and then, seeing that he had nothing to nourish them, one after the other, they took flight out over the water and into the distance.

That would make a great ending if everything really were that neat and tidy. But you know fears: they leave, but they always circle back.

I say, bring 'em on!

✠✠✠✠✠✠✠✠✠

"Silent Disciples, Shouting Stones": Jesus' Procession into Jerusalem
(Luke 19:37–40)

Occasion: Weekly chapel service during Holy Week, April 10, 2003.
Location: Perkins Chapel, Perkins School of Theology, Southern Methodist University, Dallas, Texas.

September 15, 1960: I am standing on the curb along Bridge Street in New Cumberland, Pennsylvania. I started kindergarten last week. It's fun but not this much fun. We just got here and Daddy had to park on a side street. I wish there weren't so many people. I wish I was taller. He's s'posed to be coming by any minute now. I love parades.

Palm Sunday: that's what this reminds me of! Mrs. Hefflebower had us all line up along the center aisle at church and wave our palms, and she even had us lay our sweaters out on the floor like we were expecting Jesus to come by. "The Prince of Peace," she calls him.

There he is! Everybody's cheering. In the second car. A car with no top! He's sitting up on the back. He's waving. When I saw him on television he had brown hair. Now it's blonde. They say he sails a lot. He's tan (*t*) (*t*-oilet-pottie). On TV he talks a lot about the Democratic pottie. I thought all potties were the *s*- ame!

S o *s*low, his car. I have time to run out and lay my sweater in front of the wheels on the road.

(Start to take off sweater)

But Mommy says not to run out in the street.

(Pause: Hug sweater to chest)

Besides—he's not the Prince of Peace. He's just a man who wants my Mommy and Daddy to make him the president.

(Put on coat, scarf, and gloves)

December 1990, Yardley, Pennsylvania: I am standing on the curb along Main Street. I'm freezing. We can see our breath. I'm holding my two-year-old son Matthew, who feels way heavy on one hip, and restraining my daughter Becca, age five, with my hand on her shoulder. I think she knows better than to run out in the road when he comes by, but better safe than sorry. He'll be coming by any moment. The cheers are starting up, and here's the bright red fire engine. Here's the HO! HO! HO! Here come the candy canes! Here come the squeals and the upstretched arms. I know better than to run into the road and place my coat under the wheels of his fire engine. So do my children! For one thing, it's too cold. For another thing, he's not the King of Kings. He's the king of retail!

(Take off coat, scarf, and gloves, and lay them on first pew)

The first Palm Sunday: Mothers and their children, fathers, friends, disciples, and enemies stood along the road from Bethany to Jerusalem. And here he comes, rounding the bend at the Mount of Olives, the Prince of Peace riding atop a donkey. Not campaigning, not entertaining. Still, the cheering starts up. "Blessed is the king who comes in the name of the Lord! Peace in heaven and glory in the highest heaven!" People ran to lay palm branches and their cloaks in his path, a sign of honor. Said some of the Pharisees in the crowd, "Teacher, order your disciples to stop." He replied, "I tell you, if these were silent, the stones would shout out" (Luke 19:40).

(Prop: Bamboo stick to tend pretend fire!)

The courtyard of the high priest's house, the night of his interrogation (Luke 22:54–62): I am standing by my fire in the middle of my master's courtyard. It's my job to keep burning what the guards have started. There he is. Coming by. I hate the way they are pulling and bullying him. For a flash, I picture myself running after him, throwing myself between him and his guards. Why are his disciples lagging behind him? Why aren't they defending him?

I've heard about him—only saw him once before. Yesterday, I was gathering kindling, and he was standing with several of his followers near the Temple. He was pointing to a poor old widow putting a couple of small coins in the treasury. "She has done what she could." Not many teachers commend a woman, a poor one at that! He must have felt my stare because he turned around then and looked at me and smiled.

I don't like the way most men look at me. I keep my eyes down, and I am almost glad to be too poor to own more flattering clothes. I have my "don't notice me" walk, and I try to always stay as close as possible to the exits. But for about the first time in my life a man noticing me seemed like a good thing. They shouldn't be able to drag a man like him like that.

My fire is going better, higher now. Now a man sits down and warms himself across from me. I recognize him. He is one of Jesus' disciples. I know it! I've seen him before.

Does a friend wrap a cloak tight around him at a warm fire while his friend is suffering? Some strange anger made me break my "speak only when spoken to" rule. I pointed to him and said loudly, "This man also was with him!" I may be just a servant girl, but I know the difference between a friend and a coward.

(Props: High stand with jewelry box filled with necklaces all tangled together. Put on black shawl and silver bracelet. Put shawl around shoulders.)

(As you talk, absentmindedly try to untangle necklaces.)

The chamber of Pilate's wife (Matt. 27:15–26): Why should I feel as if a knife were being twisted within me? I never even met him. I was standing by my upper window last night when they led him by on the way to Caiaphas's house for questioning. Always looking at life from behind my shutters. I had the absurd impulse to jump out, fly down, and, like a great bird, put him on my back and fly him up out of the tangle.

I tried to go to sleep at my usual time, but fell into a strange dream in which I myself sat in my husband's seat, looking into the eyes of the young prisoner, who was looking back at me with nothing but understanding. "He is innocent! He is innocent! Release him! Release him!" A voice began softly at first, then building in volume. I woke up just as I realized the voice was my own.

Why, how is it that the woman I am in my dreams takes action while the woman I am in the light of day stands to one side and watches? I sent a note straightaway to my husband: "Have nothing to do with this innocent man, for today I have suffered a great deal because of a dream about him."

They're deciding his fate now. Not too likely they'll listen to me! Still, for once I did something!

How did everything get so tangled up?

(Take off black shawl from around shoulders and place it around your head.)

A moment of Jesus' death; women at the cross (Luke 23:49, 55–56): We are standing at a distance watching. Words fail us. We keep a silent vigil, our presence a testimony to a faithfulness that is stronger than death. Now we go to prepare spices and ointments. We do what we can.

(Pause.)

Today. He'll be by soon. Every year I stand here harboring the foolish hope that, this year, the outcome will be different. His choice is not going to change. But isn't there at least the chance that ours could? Insisting on integrity? Beseeching justice? Standing in solidarity? Isn't there the chance that disciples could sustain their Hosannas all week long, and be joined in joyful chorus by the shouting stones?

(Silent symbolic action: *silently place sweater, shawl, coat, scarf, hat, and gloves on aisle to prepare for Jesus.*)

"My Favorite Angel": The Angel's Appearance to the Women at the Tomb
(Matthew 28:1–10)

Occasion: Fourth Sunday of Easter, April 13, 2008.
Location: Evening service, Episcopal Church of the Ascension, Dallas, Texas.

The angels in Matthew's Gospel remind me of my UPS man. He's very focused on his job. He is there to deliver a package, not to sell it to me. "Hey, Mrs. M. I understand your husband has seasonal allergies. Here is a humidifier from the Sharper Image. It got an excellent Consumer Report rating. There is a rebate coupon enclosed. I highly recommend it."

He's there to deliver a package, not there to be my buddy or to empathize with me. "Mrs. M, hey. How are you feeling about this humidifier? I know anxiety can be part of this process of receiving a package, and I just want to reassure you that it will be a positive addition to your home and to encourage you in the big step of accepting it into your home."

He is there to ring the doorbell, hand me the package, and hold out the clipboard for me to sign for it.

The angels in Matthew's Gospel are like my UPS man. They are focused on their job: to deliver the good news. They are not there to sell it to us. They are not there to be our buddy or to empathize with us. They're there to deliver their package: the good news. It's up to us to sign for it, open it, and use it.

The good news is only ever preceded by one short, preliminary sentence.

"Don't be afraid."

"Don't be afraid, Zechariah. Your wife Elizabeth will bear a son and you will name him John."

"Don't be afraid, Mary."

"Don't be afraid, shepherd men. I bring you good news of great joy that shall be for all people."

"Don't be afraid, Joseph, Take Mary as your wife. Her baby is conceived by the Holy Spirit. Name him Jesus. He's going to save all people from their sins."

"Don't be afraid." Then they deliver the package and you sign for it, open it, and use it.

I especially love this angel in Matthew's version of the resurrection. This is an angel who knows how to make an entrance. He comes in with a flourish! Great earthquake, just like at the death of Jesus in Matthew. This is a buff angel. He rolls back the large, sealed stone. This is an angel with attitude. After he rolls back the stone, he sits on it and crosses his angelic arms. He glances over at the guards who are displaying certain physical symptoms of extreme terror we won't go into. He doesn't tell them not to be afraid, I assume, because he doesn't care if they are afraid or not. That message he is reserving for someone else, or two someone elses.

And he rolls his eyes, as if to say "Take that, Caiaphas, take that Pilate. That's what God thinks of your effort to put the Messiah in a booth. A tomb as a prison for the Prince of Peace, the Son of God? Think again! A tomb for his final resting place? I don't think so."

Now for his main message: He turns his bright angelic eyes toward Mary Magdalene and the other Mary (whom in Matthew is probably the mother of Jesus) and here it is: "Do not be afraid. I know that you are looking for Jesus who was crucified. He is not here. He has been raised, as he said." Matthew wants to make sure we notice these three little words, "as he said."

Because in Matthew's Gospel, Jesus told you so—three times. Jesus tried to deliver the good-news package three times to the disciples in his Gospel, but they refused to sign for it. Starting in 16:21, "Jesus began to show his disciples that he must go to Jerusalem and undergo great suffering at the hands of the elders and chief priests and scribes, and be killed, and on the third day be raised." Peter's not signing for this package. "Peter took him aside and began to rebuke him, saying, 'God forbid it, Lord! This shall never happen to you!'" Peter won't sign for it; he hears the suffering part, the death part, and he doesn't even hear the "be raised" part.

In 17:22, "As they were gathering in Galilee, Jesus said to them, 'The Son of Man is going to be betrayed into human hands, and they will kill him and on the third day he will be raised.'"

But "they were greatly distressed." They wouldn't sign for it. They didn't hear the "be raised" part.

(Matt. 20:17 is the third of the three predictions. There is no response at all to Jesus' prediction by the disciples.)

Despite Jesus' repeated predictions of his "being raised," still the women came that morning, Mark and Luke tell us, with spices to anoint his dead body.

Why do we still, like them, despite the witness of Scripture, tradition, our life of worship and service, come to so many situations looking for death when we have been promised life is waiting there for us?

1. Is it because when we look to the past we see that life has dashed our high hopes? Things didn't turn out like we hoped. Circumstances went against us. Other people disappointed or hurt us.

- "You're breaking up with me now? And over the phone?"
- "I thought I was in line for that position."
- "I've watched my diet and exercised three times a week. I don't get this."
- "There were no signs that she was depressed. She baked a cake this morning."
- "Shouldn't there be a heartbeat at twelve weeks?"

Why is it that we only hear the first half of Jesus' prediction—"The Son of Man will suffer and be killed"—but forget what comes next? Why do we come to so many situations alert to signs of death, disappointment, and defeat, when we have been promised life and hope and victory is waiting there?

2. Is it because, when we look to the future, with what we know of life, we know that difficult situations lie ahead?

I was invited to the 2 by 2 Sunday school class at Highland Park UMC last Sunday. They wanted me to come teach a session on the parables. I deduced that this was a couples class of mature adults. As instructed, I arrived at 9:20, came in the side entrance, went up the stairs, and turned right. A lady, named Alice, greeted and called over another lady whose name was also Alice, and we compared notes about being Alices for a while. Looking around I noticed there were a lot more women than men. There was another lady standing to the side with a sort of pensive look on her face. I greeted her, and she brightened up a bit.

"When was the class founded?" I asked.

"Oh, years ago," she said. "But now we are all old, and lots of us are dead." Then perhaps realizing how that sounded, she added, "And we're so glad to have you with us today!"

"We're all old, and lots of us are dead."

If you are a mature adult, are you willing to sign for the good news that Jesus rose, not just died, in the face of the losses that come with increasing age?

Answer the door. It's an angel at your door with a delivery.

"Don't be afraid. He has been raised from the dead and is going ahead of you to Galilee. There you will see him. This is my message for you. Sign here."

The angel's work is done. Yours begins. Will you sign for the good news, unwrap it, and live by it?

What would that look like?

Here I invite you to brainstorm a couple of examples that would speak to you and your congregation. These would be examples of people coming into difficult situations and finding Christ's presence.

The angel's work is done. Yours begins. Will you sign for the good news, unwrap it, and live by it?

The good news is that your future is a series of situations, whether garden bowers or graveyards, where Christ awaits you to meet defeat with victory, to meet disappointment with hope, to meet death with life.

He is not here. He has been raised. Come and see the places where he lay.

✠✠✠✠✠✠✠✠

"Joseph: Father of Our Dreams": The Angel Appears to Joseph
(Matthew 1:18–25)

Occasion: Second Sunday of Advent, December 8, 1996.
Location: Langhorne UMC, Langhorne, Pennsylvania, where I served
as interim pastor, 1995–1996.

I attended a conference of teachers of preaching this past week in Santa
Fe, New Mexico. Our morning worship services were held in the historic
Loretto Chapel, a small Gothic chapel on the Old Santa Fe Trail built in
1873. It seems there is a legend about the Loretto Chapel, and it begins
like this.

When the chapel was built, the architect forgot to include a way for
the nuns to reach the choir loft. The sisters weighed their options, but all
were equally undesirable.

They could build a conventional staircase, but that would take up too
much room. They could rebuild the balcony, but that would be far too
expensive. They could climb a dangerous ladder up and down, but that
would be an accident waiting to happen. So the nuns did what you and I
should do when faced with a difficult situation. They prayed.

Their predicament reminds me of Joseph's. Swept into a situation in
which one's only choices seem to be negative ones. They talk about dilemmas having two horns: either one you sit on, you get a sore seat! Divorce
her publicly, divorce her quietly—either way, I still have to divorce her.
No way out. No possible resolution that could lead to a redemptive resolution. Only pain. It never occurred to him that Mary's unbelievable story
might be God's truth. It never occurred to him that the only thing lacking
was his embrace of that truth, and the situation would be transformed.

What do we do when we face a situation in which our only choices
appear to be negative? Agonize. Overeat. Take it out on those we love.
Try to get someone else to make up our minds for us so we can blame the
outcome on them.

No way out—only negative options. Amy Grossberg and Brian Peter-
son—eighteen-year-old college freshmen—killed their newborn because
they could see only pain, only humiliation. What would have happened,
or not happened, if they had let God be born into their situation?

A young mother, her options to stay home and feel frustrated, or to go to work and feel guilty. What other choices of attitude and action would arise if she and her husband together allowed God to be born into the situation?

I want to take a moment and be quiet, and let you reflect on a situation in your life in which you see only the negatives, no way out, no hope.

I feel for Joseph, and I'll bet you do, too—in a dilemma, his human reason able to discern only negative action options. Perhaps reading between the lines of the Bible, he had a talk with himself that went something like this.

(Soliloquy performed by Andrew States, Langhorne United Methodist Church drama coordinator)

My name is Joseph, and this has been quite a day. I am so upset. I am trying to decide what to do. I have always tried to be a good man, I am devout, I pray daily, I try to be considerate of others. I don't put on airs and talk a big game in the town square. I am a doer more than a talker, a practical man. While I am a great-grandson of the majestic King David, I don't think or talk about it, and it seems to have little to do with my present life.

If I were to sum up my character, I would say this: I always try to see the best in other people and give them the benefit of the doubt. After what happened today, I see that is not always easy to do!

About a year ago, my family and Mary's completed negotiations for us to be married. She was about thirteen, I was twenty-three. We knew of each other, but the decision that we should marry was a family one, not a personal one.

We did have to meet each other and give our consent. That was easy, once I looked into her dark, kindly eyes. I assume she felt the same. Her smile seemed genuine. Then the formal betrothal period of a year began. We were absolutely bound to one another, were known as man and wife, but could not live together. Our betrothal could be broken only by death or by divorce.

It was a difficult time for us both. A time of expectation and excitement. I would invent carpentry errands that took me by her house. She would make a wide detour with her water jar on the way to the well, and walk slowly past my shop. Sometimes we would exchange a few words and smiles at the door of my shop. Not too many or the rumors would start.

Everything was going fine, with both of us looking forward to the day we could share life together. Until this morning, that is. When she stopped by my shop and told me a tall tale. That she had been picked by God for a unique purpose, that she was with child, but that this was not because of any wrongdoing on her part. That she would be gone for a time to visit her kinswoman Elizabeth.

I choked on my hurt and anger, turned away from her, clenched my fists and pounded on my bench, skinning my knuckles. She dissolved into tears, and blurted out that she had hoped that at least I would understand. I must not think of the look in her beautiful, dark eyes when she said that. Then she ran from the shop.

I cannot believe that she has done this to me. I have been sitting here all day. I have been praying, I have even cried. For one fleeting moment, I even considered the possibility that she was telling the truth—but it is more than I can swallow. What man of you would fall for a story like this?

(Looks out over the congregation)

I can't tell you how hurt I am. It would serve her right to be publicly shamed. Why not? Nobody in town would blame me.

But I am not a vengeful man. I am a man strong within myself, not concerned with others' opinion of me. I have nothing to gain by humiliating her.

What do you think I should do?

(Looks out at congregation)

Oh, I know, this is a decision I have to make myself.

(Thinks for a long moment)

I believe I will divorce her and save her the public humiliation of accusing her of adultery. It will be a quiet matter; the sooner we get it over with the better.

I mentioned that I always try to think the best of people. How I wish I could of Mary! And of God—I confess I feel somewhat betrayed by You as well as by her. How I love her still! They say that you should never let the sun go down on your anger, but the sun is setting, and I am filled with pain. I will go to bed with my pain, and hope for sleep. Tomorrow I will send a message to Mary letting her know of my decision.

Joseph didn't stick to his resolve, did he? He's in all the crèche scenes. Many of you men have played him in the living nativity across the years.

Maybe you've seen the famous painting by Rembrandt in which the young Joseph, hair tousled, face lined with fatigue and strain, stands one shoulder thrust forward as if to protect Mary from the throng, gazing into the fire with an anxious look.

Between his decision to divorce her and his presence at her side on that night of birthing, something dramatic must have happened. What?

Our text tells us what: a night of birthing just as real as Christmas Eve. The birth of a father for the Son of God. In his sleeping state, Joseph allowed God to speak to the depths of his heart and to offer a resolution to his dilemma that his human reason had failed to discern.

On this night, as much as on Christmas Eve, an angel hovered near— whispering a message from God into Joseph's sleeping ear. The angel interrupted the nightmare visions of accusation and estrangement that played in the theater of Joseph's dreams. The angel replaced them with a manger scene and visions of a boy growing and becoming strong.

"Here," whispered the angel, "is the key that unlocks your dilemma: Believe her unbelievable story. Marry her, and become the father of God's child. He will need a father to be accepted by others as he grows to manhood. He will need, not just any father, but a father like you, capable of nurturing him, and giving him a name. Immanuel—God with us.

"He will need a father like you to teach him to take risks like the one you are about to take, for he will be tempted not to take them.

"He will need a father like you to teach him to withstand the disapproval of others, as you will soon have to withstand it.

"He will need a father like you—to teach him what to do in situations like this one, when all hope seems lost and only pain remains; to model how to believe the unbelievable good news and to walk ahead in faith.

"If you do not walk the hard road to Bethlehem, who will teach him how to climb the cruel hill to Calvary?"

In this way, I imagine the father of our Lord was born that night.

And Joseph awoke from sleep and said, "Not my will, but thine be done."

Jesus is not the only one who needs an example like Joseph. For we all struggle with tough situations and yearn for assurance from one who knows from experience that God's unbelievable good news is true! If we prayerfully ponder the example of Joseph this Advent, surely God will work in us as God worked in him.

I almost forgot to tell you the end of the legend of the nuns of Loretto Chapel. It seems that one night while the sisters were praying about their predicament, a white-bearded stranger appeared at the door of the convent asking for work. A toolbox was strapped to his burro, and he told the sisters he was a carpenter. When they told him their problem, he offered to build a spiral staircase.

His spiral staircase was an engineering feat for its time, containing thirty-three steps and two complete turns of 360 degrees with no center support. The carpenter used wooden pegs instead of nails, and his only tools were a saw, a T-square, and a hammer.

As soon as the staircase was finished, the unknown craftsman disappeared without asking to be paid. Many today believe the carpenter was, indeed, St. Joseph.

Oh, maybe it's just a legend. But I say Joseph is out and about this Advent, toolbox in hand—a model of faith in hopeful outcomes to hopeless dilemmas. Don't expect lots of conversation from him. Expect, rather, a demonstration of how to build a despair-defying staircase.

✤✤✤✤✤✤✤✤✤

"Tony, Tony, Turn Around": The Parable of the Lost Coin
(Luke 15:8–10)

Occasion: Closing worship service, North Texas Annual Conference Pastors' Retreat, October 11, 2006.
Location: Tanglewood Conference Center, Pottsboro, Texas.

(Before the Scripture reading)

Chapter 15 is the heart of Luke's Gospel, with its three parables of Lost and Found—sheep, coin, and sons—in which Jesus uses images for God that are offensive: a shepherd, a woman, and a father who has no pride.

The chapter begins with the tax collectors and sinners coming near to listen to Jesus. And the Pharisees and the scribes grumbling and saying, "This fellow welcomes sinners and eats with them." We said yesterday Jesus' parables respond to the question, "What is the kingdom of God like?" It's not under our control. It shows up when and where we least expect it. It disrupts business as usual. And probably the favorite answer of Luke's parables: "It leads to justice and joy." Several of Luke's parables emphasize repentance as a dramatic redirection of a main character's mind and purpose: the Prodigal Son, the Rich Fool, the Rich Man and Lazarus.

This parable on the other hand . . . well, let me just read it now.

Hear now the parable of the Lost Coin from Luke 15:8–10.

(Scripture reading)

"Tony, Tony, turn around. Something's lost that must be found." If you're not a former Roman Catholic, you may have never heard that prayer. I'm not, but I had a friend once who told me to try praying it when I had lost my car keys. When I've lost something crucial I'll try almost anything! It's a prayer to St. Anthony of Padua, who is believed to be the patron saint of lost items. The thirteenth-century holy man left a wealthy family to become a poor priest. The tradition of invoking St. Anthony's help in finding lost or stolen things traces back to a scene from his own life. As the legend goes, Anthony had a book of psalms that, in his eyes, was priceless. There was no printing press yet. Any book had value. This was his book of psalms, his prayerbook. Besides, in the margins he'd written all kinds of notes to use in teaching students in his Franciscan Order. A novice who had already grown tired of living a religious life decided to leave the community. Besides going AWOL, he also took Anthony's Psalter! When he went to his room to his prayer corner to pray and found it missing, Anthony prayed it would be found and returned to him.

After he prayed this prayer, the thieving novice fleeing through the forest was met by a demon (OK, this part of the story is murky—how a negative could be an avenue of God's good); anyway he told the thief to return the Psalter to Anthony and to return to the Franciscan Order, which accepted him back.

Soon after Anthony's death, people began praying through him to find or recover lost and stolen articles. A prayer to Christ, written in honor of St. Anthony shortly after his death, goes like this

> The sea obeys and fetters break
> And shattered hopes thou dost restore
> While treasures lost are found again
> When young or old thine aid implore.

The popular version of this is "Tony, Tony, turn around. Something's lost that must be found."

What lost items do people we know of pray for?

- A young man or woman who has lost a leg in Iraq, one of three hundred servicepeople wounded there in the first week of October—what do they pray will be returned to them?
- Dena Schlosser and Andrea Yates, two women who murdered their children and are now roommates at a North Texas state hospital—what do they pray will be returned to them?
- Amish parents in Lancaster County, Pennsylvania—what do they pray will be returned to their community?
- Citizens of a nation that has lost faith in its leaders, the respect of the world, and many lives . . . for what can they pray? We pray?
- Well-coifed motivational speakers who dare to call themselves preachers—long on gall and short on gospel—what do they pray will be returned to them?
- An overpaid, overhyped professional athlete—swearing on the sidelines—what lost article would you pray could be restored or returned to him if you were there with him?

So many coins clinking around on the floor of your congregation: lost hope, faith, self-esteem, perspective . . . so many lost items, so little time. A woman told me recently, "I can't stand to go into my church anymore, not since my husband's funeral there last year." If she is a member of your church, you have got to find her lost faith for her and give it back to her!

If a student comes into my office and says, "You gave me a B on my sermon instead of an A because there wasn't enough good news in it. I wanted to explain to you why. It's not that I wasn't listening in class. It's because since my miscarriage I have lost my faith." I have to find her faith for her and give it back to her. The future proclamation of the church depends on it.

We are in the business of helping people find lost items. Isn't that in our job description? To be the Good Shepherd who goes out finding those lost sheep, risking skinned knees and strained wrists as we crawl into the ravines where they have stranded themselves? Or wait, I guess we're to be the loving parental figure like Motel 6: we leave the light on for them, we keep the home-faith fires burning while they're out for a decade or so finding themselves. Isn't this our calling—to be the one charged with turning on the lights, getting out the Dirt Devil, listening for the thump that tells us a significant object has been sucked into the vac bag. Then get in there with both hands and retrieve that thing. Get out there and bring in those new members. Give those seekers what they're searching for. The music. The message. The sense of mission. Proclaim that word. Serve up that Bread of Life. But make it tasty.

In all this finding activity, what are you in danger of losing, pastor? For Luke the treasures of the life of discipleship were the habits of persistent prayer, compassion for the poor, and joy.

One Sunday morning several years ago, on my way into the church our family attended in Pennsylvania, I spotted the lost-and-found box in the entryway and decided to look through it to see if I could find my son's missing blue mitten. There was no blue mitten in it, but there was a pair of glasses in there. A set of keys. A watch. There is a lot that can show up in the lost-and-found box of your life lying in there unclaimed while you go about your ministry.

It's possible to lose a lot of things and keep on keeping on. You can lose

Direction
Faculties
Faith
Focus
Friends
Ground
Hair
Head
Heart (to someone)
Hope
Keys
Mind
Mobility
Perspective
Respect for someone
Spark
Teeth
Temper
Touch

Sometimes when you lose something, it's a good strategy to retrace your steps and find the spot where you lost it.

Revisit the mall stores where you might have left your credit card. The sink where you took off your wedding band and put it on the soap dish. Retrace your steps. Where did I mislay my communion time with God in favor of a crammed calendar? Where did we temporarily misplace our compassion for the poor in favor of programs? And where did we leave our joy in proclaiming God's word—my "Thank God Sunday's coming because I have something to say" in favor of "Sunday's coming again. . . . I have to find something to say"?

When did so much of the energy of our proclamation become finding the right illustration—rather than allowing ourselves to be found in the midst of our ministry, and proclaiming the good news out of the mundane stuff of our daily lives that the Son of Man has come to seek out and to save the lost? When your energy is all used up, gone, that's OK. Just lie in the corner and shine and God will find you. God will pick you up.

Our oldest daughter Melissa got married October 7. I performed the ceremony and hosted a houseful of out-of-town company. Superpastor. Superhostess. Supermom. In the days leading up to their arrival I became a tad frazzled. One day last week, I was running multiple errands: dry cleaners, grocery store, gas station, my most recent stop: the drive-through ATM. I pulled my money out and drove off and turned right out of the parking lot to drive home. It wasn't long before I noticed this other car coming right up behind me and beeping. *What an idiot!* I thought. *I'll bet they're drunk. And look at that, she has kids in her car. What is she thinking?* The woman drove her SUV right up beside mine and motioned for me to pull over. While holding up my ATM card.

It's not every day that something you lost comes looking for you. Your keys aren't going to suddenly stand with a dramatic jingling sound and, like Ezekiel's valley of dry bones, rise up and come to find you. That's ridiculous.

Yesterday after the session, Gifford Long came up to me and asked boldly, "How does the lost sheep repent?" I thought, *OK, this is a riddle.* Because I had been studying this passage, I knew the answer. "Well, it doesn't, except by being found!"

"That's right," he said.

I had this absurd impulse to take him aside and say to him, "Gifford, don't tell anybody else this riddle. Because it's the focus of my sermon for tomorrow's closing worship service." I didn't say that to him, because that impulse was silly. It's not like it's a secret. It's not like I'm telling a group of pastors anything you don't already know when I remind you that the emotional energy of this parable of the Lost Coin, like that of the Lost Sheep and Lost Sons that surround it, is on the Finder, on the Shepherd, the Woman, the Undignified Father. On the act of finding more than on what is lost. It's not like I'm telling a group of pastors anything you don't already know when I mention that, in this parable, repentance means allowing yourself to be found by God in the midst of your ministry.

And who knows where allowing yourself to be found will lead!

God has a hard time finding me when I'm awake. Sometimes God waits 'til I'm asleep. Seven years ago I was serving as an interim pastor at Langhorne UMC, Langhorne, Pennsylvania. It was about a six-hundred-member church. I was finishing my PhD in homiletics at Princeton Seminary, just getting started writing and dreaming about what I might contribute to writing about preaching and wisdom. I was starting to interview for positions at a couple of seminaries. The staff parish committee formally asked me to stay and become their full-time pastor on a Friday afternoon. I felt tremendous conflict between the deep, longstanding call to write and this newer pull of this local church whose people I had grown to love. I felt that staying would mean all my energies would be focused on the church and its needs and that a decision to stay would be in effect a vocational choice that would leave little time for writing amid church and family needs. That night I had a dream. I dreamed I was running. As I ran, a golden pebble slipped out of my hand and fell by the wayside. I ran on, but looked back over my shoulder. And the pebble called out to me, "Come back and get me now, or you never will."

Rabbi Eliezer in the first century taught his students, "Repent one day before your death." One of them then asked, "How will we know when that day is?" To which he replied, "All the more reason to repent today."

> The sea obeys and fetters break
> And shattered hopes thou dost restore
> While treasures lost are found again
> When young or old thine aid implore.

"Tony, Tony, turn around. Something's lost that must be found."

(_____(name various listeners, Frank, Frank, John, John, Lydia, Lydia, Anne, Anne, ending with yourself) turn around....)

✤✤✤✤✤✤✤✤✤

"Suppertime at the Gospel Café": The Christ Hymn
(Philippians 2:1–11)

Occasion: Sunday morning services, September 25, 2005.
Location: First United Methodist Church of Allen, Texas, the church my family and I attend.

Arriving at Work

Imagine that the apostle Paul (Chef Paul) has bought a restaurant. It used to be called the Heartbreak Café, but he has renamed it the Gospel Café, because he plans to serve up all kinds of spiritual nutrition. He has changed the menu; each night he offers one entrée and several sides. He pairs them carefully so that only things that go together well are on each diner's plate.

It's suppertime at the Gospel Café. The rosy tints of sunset glow in the sky around the gleaming silver diner set on a hill. You enter through the back door into the kitchen, get your apron off the hook on the wall, tie it on, and go over to stand beside Chef Paul. Because you are the newest member of the wait staff and this is your first night, he leads you to where the swinging door separates the kitchen from the dining area, pushes it open slightly, and with one arm around your shoulder, points you to a table at which eight people are seated arguing vigorously.

"We're doing a different promotion each night," Chef Paul tells you. "Tonight is free entrées for tragic heroes and heroines. You'll know most of them. All talented, almost larger than life, but all with a fatal flaw that has led or is leading to their downfall.

"You know the entrée this evening. So go find out what sides they'd like with their entrée. And come and let me know. Good luck. Here's a hint. They like to be flattered."

At the Table, Taking Orders

You wipe your sweaty palms on your apron, pull out your order pad, and head their way.

The noise is ferocious. You have to clink a fork against a glass to quiet them down.

"Hi everyone. My name is _____ and I'll be your waitress this evening. At the Gospel Café we have one entrée, and then you can have a choice from a variety of sides. The entrée this evening is the peace of God. The peace of God is free this evening. It is a hearty portion. It is also extremely healthy, resulting in unity among groups and a profound peace in the individual soul, even in bad situations.

"Down at the bottom of the menu you see the sides. You can have the peace of God with compassion, sympathy, or gentleness. I can't hear anyone if you all talk at once. Well, I'm sorry if you don't like any of those choices. If you want something different to go with your peace of God, I'll have to check with Chef Paul in the kitchen.

"Let me go around the table and find out what each of you would like to go with the peace of God.

"Mr. Russell Crowe, New Zealand native and one of my favorite actors, despite your legendary tantrums. What can I get for you? You'd like the peace of God with a side of anger. OK, I'll check on that.

"And Tonya Harding, Olympic-bound figure skater who conspired to have Nancy Kerrigan clubbed on the knee at the 1994 Olympic trials. What would you like to go with the peace of God? A side of vengeance. OK.

"And Othello, protagonist of the Shakespearean play by the same name. You suspected your wife unjustly of infidelity and murdered her in her bed. You'd like the peace of God with a side of jealousy.

"And Terrell Owens, wide receiver for the Philadelphia Eagles and, some would say, a little too fond of the fame. You would like the peace of God with a side of ego.

"President Clinton, you're looking fit after your recent surgeries. We certainly appreciate the good work you and former President Bush have done in raising money for the tsunami and hurricane relief. What can I get for you? You'd like the peace of God with a side of lack of self-control.

"And Mr. John Belushi, *Saturday Night Live* comedian of the 1970s and early 1980s, we lost you to an overdose of heroin and cocaine in 1982. You'd like the peace of God with a side of party.

"And Janis Joplin, Port Arthur native and brilliant songwriter and blues/rock singer, we lost you to an overdose on heroin in 1970 at the age of twenty-seven. You'd like the peace of God with a side of anguish.

"And Sylvia Plath, gifted American novelist and poet, everyone appreciated you but you. You never thought you were good enough and died by your own hand at the age of thirty in 1963. You'd like the peace of God with a side of perfectionism.

"And President Nixon, it's good to see you, sir. You'd like the peace of God with a side of paranoia.

"All right, thanks everyone. I'll just leave you to talk among yourselves while I go check with Chef Paul to see if he has the makings for those sides back in the kitchen."

You turn to go back to the kitchen. Immediately the noise of arguing starts up again. John Belushi says across the table to Tonya Harding, "So, how's the professional wrestling career going?"

"You wouldn't be saying that if I could reach you from where I'm sitting," she retorts.

Russell Crowe interjects, "If you two don't shut up, I'm going to throw something at you."

President Nixon turns to Janis Joplin and asks, "Why are they all talking about me?"

You poke your head out of the kitchen door, and say brightly, "Will this all be on one check?"

Tragic Heroes/Heroines: The Philippians

Tragic heroes and heroines are the same in literature and life. They are trapped in a script. Their most destructive trait jumps in the driver's seat and drives their life and their gifts right over the cliff. Churches, nations—it can happen there, too.

Paul fears the Philippians are on the drive to the cliff, sitting around the table in the fellowship hall at Philippi and arguing over whether they should confess Jesus as Lord openly since Caesar has the notion that he is Lord.

In his letter to his beloved Philippians, Paul, in prison, is serving the squabbling church a heaping portion of the peace of God. He starts the letter, "Grace to you and peace from God our Father and the Lord Jesus Christ." He ends the letter, "Do not worry about anything, but in everything by prayer and supplication with thanksgiving let your requests be made known to God. And the peace of God, which surpasses all understanding, will guard your hearts and your minds in Christ Jesus" (Phil. 4:6–7). He wants them to know the gift of the peace of God—what we have seen in people the past few weeks sitting on cots in shelters or standing in the ruins of their homes, knee high in water. As one woman said, "We don't have anything left. But we have God."

Here is Paul, sitting in prison with dried blood crusted around his ankles from the chains on them and a stench like a porta-potty a week overdue for service, the sounds of moaning, and a plate with moldy bread for dinner. Knowing that death is blowing his way, just not knowing when it will hit. And his mind is filled, not with worry about himself, but with worry about the Philippians and their spiritual state. He wants them to know the peace of God.

And it is then that the words to a hymn come to his mind.

Ad Jingles: A Theme Song for Every Situation?

Did you ever notice how TV advertisers always have a pop song to go with their product? A woman anxiously searches the mirror for crow's feet. The theme song: "I Believe in Miracles, You Sexy Thing" (L'Oreal Age Defense night cream).

A UPS man delivers a package on time. The theme song, "Don't cha worry 'bout a thing, don't cha worry 'bout a thing" (Stevie Wonder) plays in the background.

A late-model Buick Lacrosse graces the screen. "Dream on, dream on, dream on, dream until your dreams come true."

Where is the magic, make-it-all-right theme song for my friend whose son's cancer has returned, who wrote me recently, "I always feared my faith could withstand anything but losing John. I hope I don't have to find out"?

Where is the snappy tune for those whose homes, and maybe whose faith, have taken a direct hit with Katrina and now with Rita? Who are asking, "Why do bad things happen in a world supposedly ruled over by a good God?" Not yet ready to ask, "How is it that good things happen in a world of chaos and violence?"

The Christ Hymn: Paul's Theme Song for the Philippians (and for Us)

Where is the theme song for the unpeaceful Philippians? God put a song in Paul's mind and on his lips. Acts 9:25 tells us that he sang hymns in prison. The theme song the Philippians need is the Christ Hymn, the oldest Christian hymn in existence. Its theme is the mind of Christ. "Have this mind among yourselves that is yours in Christ Jesus."

I was at the tailor at the corner of McDermott and 75 last week dropping off a preaching robe I had ordered from a catalogue that needed altering. I asked the young woman tailor, "Do you think you could make a preaching robe for me sometime?"

She thought for a moment. "If you brought me a pattern," she said. "I would need for you to bring me a pattern."

Paul brings us a pattern for a life pleasing to God, filled with the peace of God: that pattern is "the mind of Christ." The mind of Christ means Christ's "habitual attitude." Christ's "disposition."

The Christ hymn is a two-act play: what Christ does, then what God does in response. Christ Jesus rid himself of the staleness of selfishness, and he filled himself with the sweet fragrance of service to others. Jesus bathed feet, bore insults, bent with anguish in the garden, and bore the cross. And it was all entirely by his own choice.

Then comes a beautiful upswing. The second half of the hymn is all about what God did. God exalted him so that the obedient one is now the one to be obeyed. God gave him the name "Jesus" derived from the Hebrew word for messiah or savior (*Yeshua*) combined with the Greek term (*kurios*) for "master," which we often render as "Lord," a title reserved for Caesar. Every knee should now bow, not to the emperor, but to Jesus Christ. Every tongue, every language on earth, should now admit openly and publicly the one they serve. Not Lord Caesar, but Lord Jesus.

We have the mind of Christ. It is a gift God offers to us on a platter of grace. But it is also a choice: it is up to us to choose to live by that pattern or not. But if we choose Christ as our pattern, God promises to help us live as Christ did. We will need help every day, for living for others rather than primarily for ourselves is not something we can naturally just do on our own steam. God's exaltation of Jesus promises that what is true for Jesus is true for Paul, for the Philippians, for us: when we take the risks involved in living for others, God will not allow the worst that life can hurl at us to permanently destroy us.

Thursday nights my husband Murry and I go out to eat while our son Matt is at soccer practice. When we got home around 8 o'clock one evening, the message light was on. Murry pushed the button, and we both stood by the phone in the family room and heard the warm, gravelly voice of his Uncle Jim. Uncle Jim was an air force meteorologist for many years. On his retirement from the air force he answered a call to ministry at age fifty-five and became a local pastor serving several small churches in north Central Texas for the next twenty years. Though his health was deteriorating due to both diabetes and emphysema, his love for God's people and his faith were growing stronger. He had a portable oxygen unit and a specially equipped van, and he made his rounds with cheerfulness and preached with all the breath he could muster. He had to retire last year from the UM church in Petrolia where he still lives.

This is your Uncle Jim. I had a biopsy last Monday and it wasn't good. There's cancer in my lymph nodes, and with my poor health, the doctor said I couldn't stand the treatments. I'm an old weatherman, so I always want an accurate prediction. So I said to the doctor, "So, doc, give me a prediction. Do I have six months?" He hesitated and then said, "Maybe four to six." So, friends, my future is where it's always been, in God's hands. I'll be home all night if you want to call.

The Christ hymn with its beautiful description of the mind of Christ is the song God puts into Paul's heart that brings him the peace that surpasses all understanding, in all circumstances, even when awaiting death in a prison cell. It is the hymn at the heart of the book of Philippians. It is the hymn Paul prays will be at the heart of First Church, Philippi, and First United Methodist Church of Allen, Texas, in your heart and at the heart of your family life.

The Christ hymn is at the heart of all these things because it expresses the very heart of God: radical, risky, self-giving love.

Breaking the (Good) News

It's suppertime at the Gospel Café. There's a table of eight tragic heroes and heroines verbally sparring while they wait for you to come back and tell them about their side orders. You've consulted with Chef Paul, and he has given you an answer to take back to them in no uncertain terms. You can't hide in the kitchen anymore. You have to go out and tell them the good news that will sound like bad news to them.

With trembling knees you approach the table. You pick up a fork and clink it against a glass.

You clear your throat and announce to them, "I asked Chef Paul about your sides. I'm sorry to have to tell you this, but he says you can't have the peace of God with anger. And you can't have the peace of God with revenge. And you can't have the peace of God with jealousy. And you can't have the peace of God with egotism or lack of self-control. And you can't have the peace of God with substance abuse, despair, perfectionism, or paranoia.

"In fact, he told me to come out here and tell you this in no uncertain terms:

"The peace of God only comes with the mind of Christ."

Appendix: For Further Reading

Writing Exercises

Bernays, Ann, and Pamela Painter. *What If? Writing Exercises for Fiction Writers.* New York: Longman, 2003.

Groff, Kent Ira. *Writing Tides: Finding Grace and Growth through Writing.* Nashville: Abingdon Press, 2007.

Rainer, Tristine. *The New Diary: How to Use a Journal for Self-Guidance and Expanded Creativity.* New York: G. P. Putnam's Sons, 1978.

Sharp, Caroline. *A Writer's Workbook: Daily Exercises for the Writing Life.* New York: St. Martin's Griffin, 2000.

Smith, Michael C., and Suzanne Greenberg. *Everyday Creative Writing: Panning for Gold in the Kitchen Sink.* Chicago: NTC Publishing, 1997.

"To Read" Lists by Novelists

Hansen, Ron, and Jim Shepard, eds. *You've Got to Read This: Contemporary American Writers Introduce Stories That Held Them in Awe.* New York: HarperCollins Perennial, 1994.

O'Brien, Geoffrey. *The Browser's Ecstasy: A Meditation on Reading.* New York: Counterpoint, 2000.

Zane, J. Peder, ed. *The Top Ten: Writers Pick Their Favorite Books.* New York: W. W. Norton, 2007.

The Art of Reading

Alter, Robert. *The Pleasures of Reading in an Ideological Age.* New York: W. W. Norton, 1996.

Calvino, Italo. *Six Memos for the Next Millennium.* New York: Random House, 1988.

Foster, Thomas C. *How to Read Literature Like a Professor.* New York: Harper Paperbacks, 2008.

O'Brien, Geoffrey. *The Browser's Ecstasy: A Meditation on Reading.* New York: Counterpoint, 2000.

Prose, Francine. *Reading Like a Writer: A Guide for People Who Love Books and for Those Who Want to Write Them.* New York: HarperPerennial, 2006.

The Art and Craft of Novel and Short-Story Writing

Bradbury, Ray. *Zen in the Art of Writing: Releasing the Creative Genius within You.* New York: Bantam Books, 1992.

Forster, E. M. *Aspects of the Novel.* New York: Harcourt, 1927.

Gardner, John. *On Becoming a Novelist.* New York: W. W. Norton, 1983.

Stanek, Lou Willett. *So You Want to Write a Novel.* New York: Quill Press, 1994.

Turchi, Peter, and Andrea Barret, eds. *The Story behind the Story: 26 Stories by Contemporary Writers and How They Work.* New York: W. W. Norton, 2004.

Welty, Eudora. *One Writer's Beginnings.* Cambridge, MA: Harvard University Press, 1984.

Wharton, Edith. *The Writing of Fiction.* 1924; repr. New York: Touchstone, 1997.

The Writing Life

Cameron, Julia. *The Artist's Way: A Spiritual Path to Higher Creativity.* New York: Penguin Putnam, 1992.

———. *The Right to Write: An Invitation and Initiation into the Writing Life.* New York: Penguin Putnam, 1998.

———. *The Vein of Gold: A Journey to Your Creative Heart.* New York: Penguin Putnam, 1996. Building on the methods she outlined in *The Artist's Way*, this book offers instruction on the creative process and more than one hundred exercises to foster creativity.

Davis, Jeff. *The Journey from the Center to the Page: Yoga Philosophies as Muse for Authentic Writing.* New York: Gotham Books, 2004. This book explores how the paths of yoga and writing naturally complement one another, and how yoga principles can genuinely improve your writing.

Friedman, Bonnie. *Writing Past Dark: Envy, Fear, Distraction and Other Dilemmas in the Writer's Life.* New York: HarperCollins, 1993.

Interviews with Novelists

Casey, Nell, ed. *Unholy Ghosts: Writers on Depression.* New York: HarperCollins, 2001.

Clark, Diana Cooper. *Interviews with Contemporary Novelists.* New York: St. Martin's Press, 1986.

LeClair, Tom, and Larry McCaffery, eds. *Anything Can Happen: Interviews with Contemporary American Novelists.* Chicago: University of Illinois Press, 1983.

Levasseur, Jennifer, and Keven Rabalais, eds. *Novel Voices: 17 Award-Winning Novelists on How to Write, Edit, and Get Published.* Cincinnati, OH: Writer's Digest Books, 2003.

Neubauer, Alexander. *Conversations on Writing Fiction: Interviews with 13 Distinguished Teachers of Fiction Writing in America.* New York: HarperCollins, 1994.

Writers Dreaming: Writers Talk about Their Dreams and the Creative Process. New York: Carol Southern Books, 1993.

The Dynamics of Creativity

Davis, Jeff. *The Journey from the Center to the Page: Yoga Philosophies and Practices as Muse for Authentic Writing.* New York: Gotham Books, 2004.
Hogue, David A. *Remembering the Future: Imagining the Past Story, Ritual, and the Human Brain.* Cleveland: Pilgrim Press, 2003.
Osborn, Alex F. *Applied Imagination: Principles and Procedures of Creative Problem-Solving.* New York: Charles Scribner's Sons, 1963.
Root-Bernstein, Robert, and Michele Root-Bernstein. *Sparks of Genius: The 13 Thinking Tools of the World's Most Creative People.* New York: Houghton Mifflin, 1999.
Turchi, Peter. *Maps of the Imagination: The Writer as Cartographer.* San Antonio, TX: Trinity University Press, 2004.
Weiner, Robert Paul. *Creativity and Beyond: Cultures, Values, and Change.* Albany: State University of New York Press, 2000.

The Craft of Screenwriting

Campbell, Joseph. *The Hero's Journey.* Novato, CA: New World Library, 2003.
Field, Syd. *Screenplay: The Foundation of Screenwriting.* New York: Bantam Dell Publishing Group, 2005.
Flinn, Denny Martin. *How Not to Write a Screenplay: 101 Common Mistakes Most Screenwriters Make.* New York: Lone Eagle, 1999.
Iglesias, Karl. *The 101 Habits of Highly Successful Screenwriters.* Cincinnati: Adams Media, 2001.
———. *Writing for Emotional Impact: Advanced Dramatic Techniques to Attract, Engage, and Fascinate the Reader from Beginning to End.* Livermore, CA: WingSpan Press, 2005.
McKee, Robert. *Story: Substance, Structure, Style, and the Principles of Screenwriting.* New York: Harper Entertainment, 1997.
Snyder, Blake. *Save the Cat: The Last Book on Screenwriting You'll Ever Need.* Studio City, CA: Michael Wiese Productions, 2005.
———. *Save the Cat Goes to the Movies: The Screenwriter's Guide to Every Story Ever Told.* Studio City, CA: Michael Wiese, 2007.
Truby, John. *The Anatomy of Story: 22 Steps to Becoming a Master Storyteller.* London: Faber and Faber, 2008.
Van Sijll, Jennifer. *Cinematic Storytelling: The 100 Most Powerful Film Conventions Every Filmmaker Must Know.* Studio City, CA: Michael Wiese, 2005.
Vogel, Christopher. *The Writer's Journey: Mythic Structures for Writers.* 3rd ed. Studio City, CA: Michael Wiese, 2007.

Notes

Introduction

1. Augustine, *On Christian Doctrine*, 1st ed., trans. D. W. Robertson Jr. (New York: Macmillan Publishing Company, 1989), 142 (4.17.34).

2. Franco-Czech novelist Milan Kundera, author of *The Unbearable Lightness of Being*, points out that "the great European novel started out as entertainment, and all real novelists are nostalgic for it! And besides, entertainment doesn't preclude seriousness.... To bring together the extreme gravity of the question and the extreme lightness of the form—that has always been my ambition" (Kundera, *The Art of the Novel* [New York: HarperCollins Publishers, 1986], 95).

3. Augustine, in commending "delight" in book 4 of *On Christian Doctrine*, went on to delineate three rhetorical "styles" in preaching: the subdued, moderate, and grand. "Delight" comes into play most strongly in the grand style where it is produced by the use of "verbal ornaments" but, more important, by the fervor of the speaker that can move listeners' emotions. In connecting imagination with delight I am moving beyond the classical understanding of metaphor from Aristotle's *Poetics* as a "verbal ornament," a figure of speech affecting individual phrases within sentences. He is fearless as a lion, or he is a lion. See Paul Ricoeur's essay "The Metaphorical Process as Cognition, Imagination, and Feeling," in *On Metaphor*, ed. Sheldon Sacks (Chicago: University of Chicago Press, 1979), 141–57.

4. Ronald E. Osborn, *Folly of God: The Rise of Christian Preaching* (St. Louis: Chalice Press, 1999), 58–59.

5. Thomas H. Troeger eloquently articulates this view in his insistence that preaching respect both "reason and rhapsody." See "The Social Power of Myth," in *Preaching as a Social Act: Theology and Practice*, ed. Arthur Van Seters (Nashville: Abingdon Press, 1988), 220–23.

6. See Barbara Brown Taylor's essay "Preaching the Body," in *Listening to the Word: Studies in Honor of Fred B. Craddock*, ed. Gail R. O'Day and Thomas G. Long (Nashville: Abingdon, 1993), 207–21.

7. The Christian apologists of the third and fourth centuries (Irenaeus, Justin Martyr, Tertullian, Clement of Alexandria, and Origen) preached sermons that countered the secret knowledge promised by various gnostic teachers.

161

The Dominicans of the thirteenth century preached teaching sermons on Christology and the sacraments to counter the gnostic theology of the Albigensians. Luther and Calvin preached teaching sermons grounded in the authority of the Bible, expounding biblical texts and themes and teaching basic beliefs to counter what they viewed as the abusive authority of the church. The German pietists of the eighteenth century preached sermons that taught about the new birth and the practicalities of daily Christian devotion to counter the Lutheran Church's sterile obsession with doctrinal purity. Many more examples could be given.

8. Robert Wuthnow, *After Heaven: Spirituality in America since the 1950s* (Berkeley: University of California Press, 1998), 2.
9. John Gardner, *On Writers and Writing* (New York: MJF Books, 1994), xvi.
10. Richard Kearney, *The Wake of Imagination: Ideas of Creativity in Western Culture* (London: Hutchinson, 1988), 3.
11. The myths perpetuated by many media images are as follows: the fittest survive; happiness consists in limitless material acquisition; consumption is inherently good; property, wealth, and power are more important than people; and progress is an inherent good (Troeger, "Social Power of Myth," 207).

Chapter 1

1. The anthology *Novel Voices* features interviews with seventeen award-winning novelists. Their notions of the purpose of fiction cover a broad spectrum. They vary from Charles Johnson, who believes a writer "interprets the world for us"; to Carrie Brown, whose purpose is "to clarify the emotional and psychological dimension of the struggle to be good"; to William Gass, who insists that "Fiction just is. It isn't supposed to do or cause anything" (Jennifer Levasseur and Karen Rabalais, eds., *Novel Voices: 17 Award-Winning Novelists on How to Write, Edit, and Get Published* [Cincinnati, OH: Writer's Digest Books, 2003], 179, 42, 113).
2. John Gardner, *On Writers and Writing* (New York: MJF Books, 1994), 221.
3. When we use the term "literature," a contemporary literary textbook tells us, we mean "compositions designed to tell stories, dramatize situations, express emotions, and analyze and advocate ideas." Literature may be classified into four categories or genres: prose fiction, poetry, drama, and nonfiction prose. While all are art forms, each has its own requirements of structure and style. Usually the first three are classified as "imaginative literature" (Edgar V. Roberts and Henry E. Jacobs, *Literature: An Introduction to Reading and Writing*, 3rd ed. [Englewood Cliffs, NJ: Prentice Hall, 1992], 3, 4).
4. The flurry of recent books on how to preach without notes reveals a cultural preference by sermon listeners for communication that, while based on careful preparation, gives the appearance of spontaneity. See Fred R. Lybrand, *Preaching on Your Feet: Connecting God and the Audience in the Preachable Moment* (Nashville, TN: B and H Academic, 2008); Joseph M. Webb, *Preaching without Notes* (Nashville: Abingdon Press, 2001); and William H. Shepherd, *Without a Net: Preaching in the Paperless Pulpit* (Limm, OH: CSS Publishing Co., 2004).
5. Gardner, *On Writers and Writing*, 223.
6. Thomas G. Long, "Out of the Loop: The Changing Practice of Preaching," in *What's the Shape of Narrative Preaching?*, ed. Mike Graves and David J. Schlafer (St. Louis: Chalice Press, 2008), 126. Long sees the contemporary trend toward preaching as instruction as symptomatic of this episodic quality of daily life.

7. David Buttrick, *Homiletic: Moves and Structures* (Philadelphia: Fortress Press, 1987), 11–12.

8. Annie Dillard, *The Writing Life* (New York: HarperPerennial, 1989), 75.

9. Julia Cameron, *The Right to Write: An Invitation and Initiation into the Writing Life* (New York: Penguin Putnam, 1998), 100.

10. Throughout its history, the novel has been subjected to the same variety of judgments as the imagination. Plato viewed the arts in general as a distraction from the search for truth, pale imitations of copies of eternal forms. Aristotle saw that imitation as creative in and of itself. See R. B. Kershner, *The Twentieth-Century Novel: An Introduction* (Boston: Bedford Books, 1997), 4. See also Italo Calvino's essay "Why Read the Classics?" in *The Uses of Literature* (New York: Harcourt Brace, 1982), 125–34. Plato's views are the origins of later assumptions by the church, both Roman Catholic and some Protestant sects, that novels were frivolous entertainment that distracts readers from proper concentration on their spiritual state (Kershner, *Twentieth-Century Novel*), 1.

11. This is the theory put forth by Ian Watt in *The Rise of the Novel: Studies in Defoe, Richardson, and Fielding* (Berkeley: University of California Press, 1957). According to Watt, the first modern novel was *Robinson Crusoe*, and the rise of the modern realistic novel was due to the rise of capitalism and its accompanying emphasis on the importance of the individual.

12. Kershner, *Twentieth-Century Novel*, 6–8.

13. Ibid., 14–16.

14. Ibid., 28.

15. Gardner, *On Writers and Writing*, 20–21.

16. Natalie Goldberg, *Writing Down the Bones: Freeing the Writer Within* (Boston: Shambhala, 2005).

17. Levasseur and Rabalais, *Novel Voices*, 171.

18. Frederick Buechner, *The Hungering Dark* (New York: Seabury Press, 1969), 50.

19. Janet Burroway with Susan Weinberg, *Writing Fiction: A Guide to Narrative Craft*, 6th ed. (New York: Longman, 2003), 9. Akira is quoted by novelist Robert Olen Butler.

20. Andre Dubus, *Meditations from a Movable Chair* (New York: Random House, 1998), 150.

21. Dillard, *Writing Life*, 68.

22. Cameron, *Right to Write*, 144.

23. Dillard, *Writing Life*, 68.

24. Joyce Carol Oates, "Preface: The Nature of Short Fiction or, The Nature of My Short Fiction," *The Writer's Digest Handbook of Short Story Writing* (Cincinnati: Writers Digest Books, 1970), xi–xii.

25. Stephen King, *On Writing: A Memoir of the Craft* (New York: Scribner, 2000), 37.

26. Ray Bradbury, *Zen in the Art of Writing* (New York: Bantam Books, 1990), 8.

27. The list is a combination of suggestions from Janet Burroway's *Writing Fiction: A Guide to Narrative Craft*, 6th ed. (New York: Longman, 2003), 13–15, and Gardner, *On Writers and Writing*, xix ff.

28. Levasseur and Rabalais, *Novel Voices*, 248.

29. Beverly Fowler Conner, "Mudslinging isn't a new trend," *Patriot News*, October 26, 2008.

30. Amy Bezecny, "Turning Fully to God," sermon on Ecclesiastes 1:1–11, submitted December 8, 2008 at Perkins School of Theology, SMU, Dallas, Texas.

31. From an interview with Michael Toms, in *The Well of Creativity* (Carlsbad, CA: Hay House, 1997), 94.

32. Quoted in *Writing Fiction*, 3.

33. Ibid., 14.

34. Levasseur and Rabalais, *Novel Voices*, 254.

Chapter 2

1. John Gardner, *On Writers and Writing* (New York: MJF Books, 1994), xix.

2. Carl Jung used the concept of archetypes (an original model of a person, ideal example, or prototype after which others are patterned) in analyzing personality and literature in the early twentieth century. His conviction was that we have an inherited memory of collective human experience that stretches back to prehistory. In fictional narratives this assumes that characters with strong archetypal features will automatically resonate with large audiences. The work of Joseph Campbell in archetypes in ancient mythology and modern narratives is well known, as expressed in his *The Hero with a Thousand Faces.*

3. *Anything Can Happen: Interviews with Contemporary Novelists*, conducted by and edited by Tom LeClair and Larry McCaffery (Chicago: University of Illinois Press, 1983), 255.

4. John Gardner, *On Writers and Writing* (New York: MJF Books, 1994), xix.

5. I am thinking especially of Patricia Wilson Kastner, Paul Scott Wilson, Frank Thomas, Nora Tubbs Tisdale, and Justo González and Pablo Jiménez.

6. Karl Iglesias, *Writing for Emotional Impact* (Livermore, CA: WingSpan Press, 2005), 26.

7. Ibid., 27.

8. Diana Cooper-Clark, *Interviews with Contemporary Novelists* (New York: St. Martin's Press, 1986), 96–97.

9. Susan Neville, "Where's Iago?" in *Bringing the Devil to His Knees: The Craft of Fiction and the Writing Life*, ed. Charles Baxter and Peter Turchi (Ann Arbor: University of Michigan Press, 2001), 34.

10. Ibid., 37.

11. Ibid., 36.

12. Ibid., 39.

13. Patrick D. Miller Jr., *Interpreting the Psalms* (Philadelphia: Fortress Press, 1986), 94.

14. Neville, "Where's Iago?" 34.

15. Janet Burroway, *Imaginative Writing: The Elements of Craft* (New York: Penguin Academics, 2007), 80–81.

16. Ibid., 81

17. John Gardner, *On Writers and Writing* (New York: MJF Books, 1994), xviii, xvi.

18. Quoted by Annie Dillard, *The Writing Life* (New York: HarperPerennial, 1989), 68.

19. John Gardner, *On Becoming a Novelist* (New York: W. W. Norton, 1983), 30.

20. Jennifer Levasseur and Kevin Rabalais, eds., *Novel Voices: 17 Award-Winning Novelists on How to Write, Edit, and Get Published* (Cincinnati, OH: Writer's Digest Books, 2003), 248.

21. Gardner, *On Becoming a Novelist*, 30.

22. Ibid., 32.

23. Josip Novakovich, *Fiction Writers' Workshop* (Cincinnati: Story Press, 1995), 49.

24. B. K. Kershner, *The Twentieth-Century Novel: An Introduction* (Boston: Bedford Books, 1997), 18.

25. Gardner, *On Becoming a Novelist*, 40.

26. Eudora Welty, *One Writer's Beginnings* (Cambridge, MA: Harvard University Press, 1984), 13–14.

27. Ibid., 14.

28. Ibid., 37.

29. Ibid., 36.

30. Levasseur and Rabalais, *Novel Voices*, 99–100.

31. Quoted by Ronald B. Tobias, *20 Master Plots: And How to Build Them* (Cincinnati, OH: Writer's Digest Books, 1993), 31.

32. Ibid., 19–30.

33. Charles Baxter and Peter Turchi, eds., *Bringing the Devil to His Knees: The Craft of Fiction and the Writing Life* (Ann Arbor: University of Michigan Press, 2001), 47.

Chapter 3

1. Annie Dillard, *The Writing Life* (New York: HarperPerennial, 1989) 12.

2. Eudora Welty, *One Writer's Beginnings* (Cambridge, MA: Harvard University Press, 1984), 84–85.

3. Janet Burroway with Susan Weinberg, *Writing Fiction: A Guide to Narrative Craft*, 6th ed. (New York: Longman Press, 2003), 4.

4. Janet Burroway, *Imaginative Writing: The Elements of Craft*, 2nd ed. (New York: Penguin Academics, 2007), xxvi.

5. Interview with Gail Godwin, from Alexander Neubauer, *Conversations on Writing Fiction: Interviews with 13 Distinguished Teachers of Fiction Writing in America* (New York: HarperPerennial, 1994), 138–39.

6. Jennifer Levasseur and Kevin Rabalais, eds., *Novel Voices: 17 Award-Winning Novelists on How to Write, Edit, and Get Published* (Cincinnati, OH: Writer's Digest Books, 2003), 160.

7. Quote appears in Michael Toms, ed., *The Well of Creativity* (Carlsbad, CA: Hay House, 1997), 5.

8. Natalie Goldberg, *Writing Down the Bones: Freeing the Writer Within* (Boston: Shambhala, 2005), 186.

9. Troeger sees the late twentieth century emphasis on narrative and imagery as an outgrowth of postmodernism's acknowledgment that theological concepts arise out of and are answerable to specific contexts. He calls us to be aware of the ways in which our own context has caused the focus of our imaginations to have become self-seeking and constricted.

10. Tom LeClair and Larry McCaffery, eds., *Anything Can Happen: Interviews with Contemporary Novelists* (Chicago: University of Illinois Press, 1983), 131, 223.

11. Robert Olen Butler, *From Where You Dream: The Process of Writing Fiction*, ed. and with an introduction by Janet Burroway (New York: Grove Press, 2005), 27.

12. Jolyon P. Mitchell, *Visually Speaking: Radio and the Renaissance of Preaching* (Edinburgh: T. & T. Clark, 1999), 55.

13. Antonya Nelson, "The Domestic Battlefield," in *Novel Voices*, 218.

14. Ibid., 8–9. See Julia Cameron's *The Vein of Gold: A Journey to Your Creative Heart*, "Your Mode of Transportation: Walking" (New York: Penguin Putnam Inc., 1996), 25–31.
15. *Well of Creativity*, 7–8.

Chapter 4

1. Edith Wharton, *The Writing of Fiction* (New York: Touchstone Books, 1997), 22.
2. Ibid., 24.
3. Ibid., 23.
4. Laurence Perrine and Thomas R. Arp, *Literature: Structure, Sound and Sense*, 6th ed. (Fort Worth, TX: Harcourt Brace College Publishers, 1993), 3–4.
5. Edgar V. Roberts and Henry E. Jacobs, *Literature: An Introduction to Reading and Writing*, 3rd ed. (Englewood Cliffs, NJ: Prentice Hall, 1992), 3–4.
6. Nancy Kress, *Dynamic Characters: How to Create Personalities That Keep Readers Captivated* (Cincinnati, OH: Writer's Digest Books, 1998), 31.
7. Ibid., 31–32. Kress includes a helpful set of questions for novelists about settings on p. 34.
8. I'll say more about the throughline in the "Preventive Medicine" section later in the book. See Nancy Kress, *Beginnings, Middles and Endings* (Cincinnati, Ohio: Writer's Digest Books, 1993), 66.
9. Janet Burroway with Susan Weinberg, *Writing Fiction: A Guide to Narrative Craft*, 6th ed. (New York: Longman, 2003), 6. Burroway directs us toward Gabriele Rico's book *Writing the Natural Way* for a full description of the method.
10. Burroway and Weinberg, *Writing Fiction*, 33.
11. Ibid., 34.
12. Jennifer Levasseur and Kevin Rabelais, eds., *Novel Voices: 17 Award-Winning Novelists on How to Write, Edit, and Get Published* (Cincinnati, OH: Writer's Digest Books, 2003), 209.
13. F. A. Rockwell, "Making the Scene," in *Handbook of Short Story Writing*, Preface by Joyce Carol Oates (Cincinnati, OH: Writer's Digest Books, 1970), 81–82.
14. *The Writer's Digest Handbook of Short Story Writing* (Cincinnati, OH: Writer's Digest Books, 1970).
15. Raymond Obstfeld, *Novelist's Essential Guide to Crafting Scenes* (Cincinnati, OH: Writer's Digest Books, 2000), 2.
16. Ibid., 3.
17. Ibid., 7–8.
18. Skip Press, *The Complete Idiot's Guide to Screenwriting* (Indianapolis: Alpha Books, 2001), 221.
19. Karl Iglesias, *Writing for Emotional Impact: Advanced Dramatic Techniques to Attract, Engage, and Fascinate the Reader from Beginning to End* (Livermore, CA: WingSpan Press, 2005), 125.
20. Terry Rossio, "Death to Readers: Screenwriting Column 05," http://www.wordplayer.com/columns/wp05.Death.to.Readers.html.
21. Robert C. Dykstra, *Discovering a Sermon: Personal Pastoral Preaching* (St. Louis: Chalice Press, 2001), 44.
22. See Sondra Willobee, *The Write Stuff: Crafting Sermons That Capture and Convince* (Louisville, KY: Westminster John Knox Press, 2009). In part 3, the author describes how to make colorful, concrete language choices in sermons. See also Oakley Hall,

How Fiction Works: Proven Secrets to Writing Successful Stories That Hook Readers and Sell (Cincinnati, OH: Story Press, 2001), esp. chap. 3, "Words."

23. Steven Schwartz, "Finding a Voice in America," in *Bringing the Devil to His Knees: The Craft of Fiction and the Writing Life*, ed. Charles Baxter and Peter Turchi (Ann Arbor: University of Michigan Press, 2001), 49.

24. Ibid.

25. Chuck Wachtel, "Behind the Mask: Narrative Voice in Fiction," in *Bringing the Devil to His Knees*, 66.

26. Burroway and Weinberg, *Writing Fiction*, 31.

27. Ibid.

28. Ibid., 32.

29. Eugene Lowry, *The Homiletical Plot: The Sermon as Narrative Art Form* (Atlanta: John Knox Press, 1980) introduced preachers to this insight.

30. Eugene L. Lowry, *How to Preach a Parable: Designs for Narrative Sermons* (Nashville: Abingdon Press, 1989), 23–26. In using the term "narrative" in relation to sermons, Lowry doesn't mean that sermons ought to be "chock full of stories or . . . to be one long story." The term "narrative" can refer to two things: First, it can refer to a particular story. Second, it can refer to "the underlying thread or plot line typical of oral narration." In the second sense, "narrative" is a sequence or form—of opening conflict, escalation, reversal, and proleptic closure. A sermon can be a narrative sermon in the sense of having a narrative form or flow "whether it follows a single story or includes several short anecdotes or illustrations" (25). Lowry says that the dual use of the term "medicine" (as a field and as a particular medication) is analogous to the dual use of "narrative" as plotline and as a particular story.

31. Madison Smartt Bell, *Narrative Design: Working with Imagination, Craft, and Form* (New York: W. W. Norton, 1997), 22.

32. Ibid., 216.

33. David Schlafer, *Surviving the Sermon* (Boston: Cowley Publications, 1992), 66. On linear versus nonlinear plots, see Josip Novakovich's *Writing Fiction Step by Step* (Cincinnati, OH: Story Press, 1998), 42–71.

34. E. M. Forster, *The Art of the Novel* (New York: Harcourt, 1927), 26.

35. John Gardner, *On Becoming a Novelist* (New York: W. W. Norton, 1983), 33.

36. Josip Novakovich, *Fiction Writer's Workshop* (Cincinnati: Story Press, 1995), 179

37. Iglesias, *Writing for Emotional Impact*, 139.

38. Ibid., 179.

39. Kress, *Dynamic Characters*, 10. In chapter 15 of *Dynamic Characters*, Kress offers "The Intelligence Dossier: A Wrap-Up System for Investigating Your Character." She presents a questionnaire for an author to fill out with information about his character. It covers basic background information, preferences and mannerisms, social ties, daily schedule, and inner life. It would be a helpful exercise to apply to preaching on biblical characters.

40. Lavonne Mueller and Jerry D. Reynolds, *Creative Writing: Forms and Techniques* (Lincolnwood, IL: National Textbook Company, 1990), 103.

41. Janet Burroway, *Imaginative Writing: The Elements of Craft*, 2nd ed. (New York: Penguin Academics, 2007), 3.

42. Natalie Goldberg, *Writing Down the Bones: Freeing the Writer Within* (Boston: Shambhalo, 2005), xiii.

43. Ibid., 7.

44. Wharton, *Writing of Fiction*, 61–62.

45. Burroway, *Imaginative Writing*, 5.

46. Ibid., 6.

47. Ibid.

48. Mueller and Reynolds, *Creative Writing*, 118.

49. See my *Preaching Biblical Wisdom in a Self-Help Society* (Nashville: Abingdon Press, 2004) for a discussion of the nuances of the relationship between these ways of thinking and biblical wisdom literature's insights on facing adversity with faith in God.

50. Burroway and Weinberg, *Writing Fiction*, 40.

51. Iglesias, *Writing for Emotional Impact*, 117. Sometimes the story begins with the inciting event and fills in the information needed in act 1 through flashbacks.

52. Nancy Kress, *Beginnings, Middles and Endings* (Cincinnati, OH: Writer's Digest Books, 1993), 7.

53. Robert McKee, *Story: Substance, Structure, Style, and the Principles of Screenwriting* (New York: HarperCollins Books, 1997), 141.

54. Raymond Obstfeld, *Novelist's Essential Guide to Crafting Scenes* (Cincinnati, OH: Writer's Digest Books, 2000), 28–29.

55. Debra Spark, "Getting In and Getting Out: First Words on First (and Last) Words," in *Bringing the Devil to His Knees: The Craft of Fiction and the Writing Life*, ed. Charles Baxter and Peter Turchi (Ann Arbor: University of Michigan Press, 2001), 107.

56. Ibid., 108–9.

57. Josip Novakovich, *Fiction Writer's Workshop* (Cincinnati, OH: Story Press, 1995), 151–65.

58. F. A. Rockwell, "How Not to Fizzle a Finale," in *The Writer's Digest Handbook of Short Story Writing* (Cincinnati, OH: Writer's Digest Books, 1970), 188.

59. Quoted in Mueller and Reynolds, *Creative Writing*, 166.

60. Rockwell, "How Not to Fizzle a Finale," 184.

61. Ibid., 188.

62. Ibid., 185.

63. Ibid. Rockwell calls this the "ideological ending," which doesn't, in my view, express the concept of open-endedness very accurately. I've renamed it the "go figure" ending.

64. Alyce M. McKenzie, *The Parables for Today* (Louisville, KY: Westminster John Knox Press, 2007), 97.

65. Frank A. Dickson and Sandra Smyth, eds., *The Writer's Digest Handbook of Short Story Writing*, with a Preface by Joyce Carol Oates (Cincinnati, OH: Writer's Digest Books, 1970), 186.

Chapter 5

1. Charles L. Rice, *Interpretation and Imagination: The Preacher and Contemporary Literature* (Philadelphia: Fortress Press, 1970), 5. Rice includes sermons on contemporary plays and movies to illustrate the dialogue he's advocating between preachers and contemporary writers. They include Lorraine Hansbury's play *A Raisin in the Sun* (1959), Richard Selig's poem "From the Sixteenth Floor" (1965), William Faulkner's novel *The Sound and the Fury*, (1929), and the movie *Easy Rider* (1969).

2. Ibid., 21.

3. See Paul Tillich's *Theology of Culture* (New York: Oxford University Press, 1959).

4. Rice, *Interpretation and Imagination*, 35.

5. Fred B. Craddock, *As One without Authority* (Nashville: Abingdon Press, 1979), 78–79.

6. Ibid., 92–97.

7. Patricia Wilson-Kastner, *Imagery for Preaching* (Minneapolis: Fortress Press, 1989), 68.

8. Ibid.

9. Ibid., 69.

10. Ibid., 77.

11. Ibid., 79.

12. Ibid., 83.

13. Ibid., 81–82.

14. Eunjoo Mary Kim, *Preaching the Presence of God: A Homiletic from an Asian American Perspective* (Valley Forge, PA: Judson Press, 1999), 72.

15. Ibid., 121–25.

16. See Ronald Y. Nakasone, "Sermon Notes for a Forty-nine Day Memorial Service," in *Ethics of Enlightenment: Essays and Sermons in Search of a Buddhist Ethic* (Fremont, CA: Dharma Cloud Publishers, 1990), 85–89, as described in Kim, *Preaching the Presence of God*, 123–24.

17. Buttrick's specific prescriptions for building moves are set out in detail in his textbook *Homiletic: Moves and Structures* (Philadelphia: Fortress Press, 1987).

18. Ibid., 14.

19. Ibid., 123.

20. Ibid., 89.

21. Ibid., 139.

22. David Buttrick, "Up against the Powers That Be," in *A Chorus of Witnesses: Model Sermons for Today's Preacher*, ed. Thomas G. Long and Cornelius Plantinga Jr. (Grand Rapids: William B. Eerdmans, 1994), 218–24.

23. Richard L. Eslinger, *Narrative Imagination: Preaching the Worlds That Shape Us*, 60. "Images may also relate to other than a visual modality. In addition to visual imaging, Edward Casey reminds us, there must be listed, 'audializing, smelling in the mind's nose, feeling in the mind's muscles, tasting in the mind's tongue and so on." Eslinger is drawing on Edward S. Casey's *Imaging: A Phenomenological Study* (Bloomington, IN: Indiana University Press, 1976), 41.

24. Ibid., 102.

25. Ibid., 90–94.

26. Ibid., 85–89.

27. Ibid.

28. Ibid.

29. Henry H. Mitchell, *Black Preaching: The Recovery of a Powerful Art* (Nashville: Abingdon, 1990), 31.

30. Henry H. Mitchell, *Celebration and Experience in Preaching* (Nashville: Abingdon Press, 1990), 37.

31. Says Mitchell, "This is old hat in Black tradition, in which it is common to hear a preacher declare that he or she saw John on the Isle of Patmos, early one Sunday morning" (ibid., 89).

32. Ibid., 39.

33. Ibid., 55.

34. Ibid., 79–82.
35. This sermon is found in ibid., 127–31.
36. Frank A. Thomas, *They Like to Never Quit Praisin' God: The Role of Celebration in Preaching* (Cleveland: United Church Press, 1997), 33.
37. This sermon was preached in May 2007 at the Mississippi Boulevard Disciples of Christ Church, Memphis, Tennessee.
38. Thomas, *They Like to Never Quit Praisin' God*, 64–67.
39. Ibid., 38–39.
40. Ibid., 39, 40.
41. Ibid., 44.
42. Ibid., 35.
43. Paul Scott Wilson, *The Four Pages of the Sermon: A Guide to Biblical Preaching* (Nashville: Abingdon Press, 1999), 11.
44. Ibid., 158.
45. Ibid., 86–87.
46. Ibid., 96–100.
47. This sermon appears in *Patterns of Preaching: A Sermon Sampler*, ed. Ronald J. Allen (St. Louis: Chalice Press, 1998), 82–86.
48. Nora Tubbs Tisdale, *Preaching as Local Theology and Folk Art* (Minneapolis: Fortress Press, 1997), 46.
49. Ibid., 47.
50. Ibid., 65–77.
51. Ibid., 43.
52. Ibid.
53. Ibid., 111–14.
54. Ibid., 114–16.
55. Ibid., 117.
56. Ibid., 117–19.
57. Ibid., 119.
58. Stephen Farris, in his book *Preaching that Matters: The Bible and Our Lives* (Louisville, KY: Westminster John Knox Press, 1998), identifies this as the process of "creative analogy." He offers guidance for making analogies between our congregation's and the text's worldviews. He also offers a crucial caution against making facile analogies that undermine the gospel message (17–18).
59. Justo L. González and Pablo Jiménez, *Pulpito: An Introduction to Hispanic Preaching* (Nashville: Abingdon Press, 2005), 46. The term *mestizaje* applies to people of mixed European and Amerindian ancestry in Latin America.
60. Ibid., 73–80.
61. Eugene L. Lowry, *The Sermon: Dancing the Edge of Mystery* (Nashville: Abingdon Press, 1997), 28.
62. Ibid., 106.
63. David Schlafer, *Surviving the Sermon* (Boston: Cowley Publications: 1992), 66.
64. Lowry, *Sermon*, 79–80, 110–11.
65. Ibid., 79.
66. Ibid., 78.
67. Eugene L. Lowry, "A Knowing Glimpse," in *Patterns of Preaching: A Sermon Sampler*, ed. Ron Allen (St. Louis: Chalice Press, 1998), 95–97.

68. Linda Clader, *Voicing the Vision: Imagination and Prophetic Preaching* (Harrisburg, PA: Morehouse Publishing, 2003), 5–6.

69. Ibid., 5.

70. Ibid., 100.

71. Ibid., 104–8.

72. Ibid., 156–58. This sermon was preached in All Saints Chapel, Church Divinity School of the Pacific, at a Eucharist incorporating the twelve steps of Alcoholics Anonymous, May 6, 1999.

73. Stephen Vincent Deleers, *Written Text Becomes Living Word: The Vision and Practice of Sunday Preaching* (Collegeville, MN: Liturgical Press, 2004), 127.

74. J. Sergius Halvorsen, in *Preaching at the Double Feast: Homiletics for Eucharistic Worship*, ed. Michael Monshau (Collegeville, MN: Liturgical Press, 2006), 114–16.

75. J. Sergius Halvorsen, "The Context of the Eucharistic Liturgy" in *Preaching at the Double Feast*, 119.

76. Mary Ann Wiesemann-Mills, "Preaching in the Context of 'Doing the Liturgy,'" in *Preaching at the Double Feast*, 168.

77. Walter Brueggemann, *Finally Comes the Poet: Daring Speech for Proclamation* (Minneapolis: Fortress Press, 1989), 109–10, cited in *Preaching at the Double Feast*, 168.

78. Linda Clader, "The Formation of a Eucharistic Preacher," in *Preaching at the Double Feast*, 218.

79. Mike Graves, *The Fully Alive Preacher* (Louisville, KY: Westminster John Knox Press, 2006), 116–19.

80. Ibid., 119. Graves's sequencing plan reminds me of something J. Barrie Shepherd says in his book *Whatever Happened to Delight?* He quotes hockey player Wayne Gretsky in an interview when he said, "Most hockey players skate to where the puck is. I skate to where it's going to be." That's what beginning with the end in mind is about; it's a way of giving our people "something to stretch for, to grow into, to skate toward" (J. Barrie Shepherd, *Whatever Happened to Delight? Preaching the Gospel in Poetry and Parables* [Louisville, KY: Westminster John Knox Press, 2006], 75).

81. A number of homileticians over the past twenty-five years have advocated text-shaped preaching across a wide spectrum of genres based on the conviction that sermons can be formed to convey, not just what the text says, but how it says it. My own work with preaching on proverbial wisdom falls within the category of genre-shaped sermons. See also Mike Graves, *The Sermon as Symphony: Preaching the Literary Forms of the New Testament* (Valley Forge, PA: Judson Press, 1997); David L. Bartlett, "Texts Shaping Sermons," in *Listening to the Word: Studies in Honor of Fred B. Craddock*, ed. Gail R. O'Day and Thomas G. Long (Nashville: Abingdon Press, 1993), chap. 8; and John C. Holbert, *Preaching Old Testament: Proclamation and Narrative in the Hebrew Bible* (Nashville: Abingdon Press, 1991), esp. chap. 3, "Reading the Bible's Narrative."

82. Thomas G. Long, *Preaching and the Literary Forms of the Bible* (Louisville, KY: Westminster/John Knox Press, 1989), 23–39.

83. Ibid., 61–65.

84. Webb has served as professor of both communication and homiletics at Pepperdine University and Claremont School of Theology. At the time of this writing, he is the Dean of the School of Communication and Media and Professor of Global Media and Communications at Palm Beach Atlantic University.

85. Joseph M. Webb, *Preaching for the Contemporary Service* (Nashville: Abingdon Press, 2006), 5.
86. Ibid., 66.
87. Ibid., 91.
88. Webb, *Preaching without Notes* (Nashville: Abingdon, 2001), 48. Another helpful book on this same subject is William H. Shepherd, *Without a Net: Preaching in the Paperless Pulpit* (Lima, OH: CSS Publishing, 2004). Shepherd offers excellent advice about choosing vivid, concrete, memorable language that is easy for the preacher to recall and hard for listeners to forget: "Make every sentence touch, taste, see, smell and hear" (108). Instead of "Christianity is about compassion," try "Christianity is one human hand reaching out to another" (109).
89. Webb, *Preaching for the Contemporary Service*, esp. chap. 1, "Contemporary Preaching as Improvisation," 13–33.
90. See Eddie Gibbs and Ryna K. Bolger, *Emerging Churches: Creating Christian Community in Postmodern Cultures* (Grand Rapids: Baker Academic, 2005), 115.
91. Ibid., 175.
92. "Preaching to Postmoderns, An Interview with Brian McLaren," in *Preaching with Power: Dynamic Insights from Twenty Top Pastors*, ed. Michael Duduit (Grand Rapids: Baker Books, 2006), 123. In McClaren's view, the dominant thing that we have to prove to a spiritually seeking non-Christian in a postmodern world is not that Christianity is true. We have to prove that it is good and beautiful. In a time of media barrage, it is not enough that we speak louder. We need to speak more beautifully. We need to speak with more passion and intensity, not necessarily more volume (124–26).
93. Ibid., 130.
94. Ibid. In some emerging churches, the sermon is a running commentary with discussion. The themes to be addressed are decided by a group, not just the pastor. A prominent example is Doug Pagitt's (Solomon's Porch, Minneapolis) dialogical sermon strategy described on p. 165 of Gibbs and Bolger, *Emerging Churches*. In still other emerging churches, teaching does not occur in the service at all. The pastor's blog is his or her pulpit.

Chapter 6

1. To mark the change of scenes, I announce them as I move through the sermon.

Index